BAD LUCK BABY

by Sun Fannin

With Love
Sun Fannin

Destiny Image Publishers
P.O. Box 351
Shippensburg, PA 17257

All names other than family are fictious to protect others

Acknowledgments

I want to thank Susan Engle for the hours she spent in listening to my life story and writing the book.

My thanks, also, to my sister-in-law, Claudia Kelton, for editing the first draft of the manuscript and offering helpful suggestions concerning grammar, style and arrangement.

Thanks to Donna McElhany for taking time from her busy schedule to type the manuscript.

Heartfelt thanks to all the people who helped, prayed and stood behind me in getting this book printed.

Most of all, my thanks to God for working out all the details related to the writing of this book. Without the beautiful flow of His anointing, and the ability He granted through His grace, the book could not have been completed.

To my Lord and Savior, Jesus Christ, Who loved me so much that He died for me to give me a brand-new life.

To my husband, Larry, who was always patient and understanding during the many hours I spent on the book.

To my boys, Jody and TeJay, who sacrificed time away from me.

To my mother, Lee, who has been supportive in prayer.

To my sister, Ann, who has always been so faithful and loving through my hardships and good times, too.

Preface

If I were to tell you that writing this book has been a simple project, I would not be honest. It has been a tremendous undertaking and one of the most challenging assignments I have ever accomplished. Many hours of arduous work were required.

This project enabled me to know Sun in a new way. One hot summer night, in particular, was a taxing time for Sun as she related a number of horrid experiences. Her husband and two sons were in bed and all was quiet, except for the sounds of her weeping and her wrenching sobs that came as Sun relived her painful past.

It nearly broke my heart to watch this precious woman, sitting cross-legged on the floor, so torn up inside, and gasping for air as she wept. I felt so helpless to comfort her; she was so caught up in her past. At times, I wondered whether or not to continue for the night, although I realized her tears were like a healing balm to her soul which had been so scarred and wounded from distressful hurts from years ago.

Sun continued to trudge along past midnight that evening as I listened intently and in amazement. There were times when I had to turn my head in revulsion as she related the cruel treatment she had received from people and the times she miraculously escaped death.

As you read the moving account of Sun's life, your heart will be deeply touched by the affliction and emotional torture she suffered. It was a miracle of God that any human being could have survived all the trauma that Sun endured.

She is living proof of a life-changing God who can take a no-good "bad-luck baby" and transform her into a priceless, blessed woman of great worth. Sun is a living miracle.

Susan K. Engle
Morristown, IN. 46161

Foreword

To personally know Sun Fannin has been and is a tremendous blessing for my wife and me. Simply to be around her builds within you a sense of joy and great expectancy. Her faith in God and her love for people shine forth as the glory of the Lord radiates from her. Wherever she is and whatever she does is for the glory of the Lord. The spirit of intercession that moves her to prayer and fasting for long periods of time is revealed in answers and miracles.

You are about to embark on a life-changing experience. Why? Because you haven't selected this book by chance or coincidence, but by Divine appointment.

What appears to be impossible becomes possible in Sun's life, bringing you to the realization that nothing is impossible with God. You will get to know Sun's heart of faith as she takes you through her life of rejection and deprivation to the total victory she now knows through Jesus Christ. Her testimony is unique, but it is also one that relates to many people today. Her openness and honesty in revealing the deepest things that have happened in her life will leave you with a new understanding of the depth of the love of God.

While you are reading you will be aware of the cleaning, healing power of the Holy Spirit moving deep within your spirit, delivering you from the hurts you have suffered. You will know, without any shadow of doubt, the life-changing, life-transforming experiences that have brought Sun to where she is today.

Yes, this book was written by the Person of the Holy Spirit abiding within Sun. The hurts she experienced were too deep to be revealed by the natural mind but could only be revealed by the mind of God. The cruelty of rejection can be dealt with and can be conquered. From her infancy to womanhood and motherhood you will see how this cruel spirit of rejection tried to destroy Sun. You will also see the staying, keeping power of a merciful and loving God working in Sun's life to bring her forth triumphant. You will see Sun's mother, brother and sisters torn and ravaged by this sinister power of darkness, followed by the light shining forth and deliverance bringing healing to her family.

This book is for you and for others you know. It is for every hurting, bleeding, precious soul. My prayer for you, as you read Sun's story, is that the Spirit of Wisdom and Revelation in the knowledge of Him will be upon you and that the eyes of your understanding will be enlightened, that you may receive what God has purposed for you.

Joe Turnbloom - International Director,
Full Gospel Business Men Fellowship International

Introduction

During the winter and spring of 1986, the desire to write became a seed planted inside me. As the weeks wore on, the intensity to write began to grow, yet I was not certain of which direction to take. I pondered whether I was to write a book on my life story, share teachings from the Lord, or keep a log of my experiences with the Lord. As a school teacher I have free time during the summer months — time I could use for writing — but what did the Lord want me to write about?

At the same time, Sun Fannin, my pastor's wife, who had come from Korea, was contemplating who she should get to help her write her story. Would it be a Korean, a professional writer, or someone outside of the church fellowship where she and her husband, Larry, serve? Before long, we both discovered the direction we were to take.

One Sunday morning, before our church service began, Sun and I were sharing with each other what the Lord had been saying to each of us. Sun shared her desire to have someone write her life story; unknown to me she had been carrying this desire for the last few years. She continued by telling me that the Lord had spoken my name to her. At that moment, I knew why I felt so strongly impelled to write. I knew by God's grace and ability I would be enabled to accomplish the task that lay ahead.

Sun and I have known each other for seven years. She has been my close friend, a confidante, a prayer partner, a sister in the Lord, and a great encourager. I have seen the Lord change and mold Sun into His image, as she has grown from glory to glory, seizing the prize of the high calling, and being an example to others. Sun's life causes me to want to emulate her.

Contents

1

"Bad-Luck Baby"

The human spirit, in some unique individuals, has a power to survive, overcome, and be victorious. It is greater than the cruelty of rejection and pain and even the authority of death.

This is the story of such an extraordinary person—a victim of great rejection and sorrow who was able to overcome and be victorious. Sun Fannin, a little Korean woman, survived much heartache and separation from the ones she needed most.

Her older sister, Ann, has provided us with an honest account of years of Sun's life. Ann never thought she would see her sister again, but because of God's grace and mercy in their lives, the two sisters were reunited.

Ann's story starts in August of 1950:

"The bombing and screaming was deafening in our city of Seoul, Korea. The noise of people running for their lives could be heard inside our home. Chaos and destruction were all around us.

"There were seven people in our family and another one was on the way. How could we possibly survive in the hell that existed all around us? Would we even be alive this time tomorrow? The continuation of life could not be guaranteed.

"Father was full of fear and anxiety, not knowing where to turn. He knew our family was in great danger, but where could he find safety? He decided he would escape the terror by finding a refuge in the nearby hills. With so much despair and uncertainty, father fled from his family and home and made his way toward the hills, but he never arrived at his destination. Father was killed during one of the countless air raids.

"My family, thinking death awaited them, became hysterical in their hopelessness. How could we survive without father?

"Mother, now a widow and eight months pregnant, already had five children to raise. She left us alone to look for Father. We then began to search for mother and found her beside father's dead body. Mother could show no emotion, nor shed tears, because she was in great shock at the loss of father. Feeling emotionally stunned and mentally numb, my mother buried her beloved up in the hills.

"With my father gone, poverty set in. As if we did not have enough mouths to feed, five weeks after father's death mother gave birth to a five-pound, black-haired, scrawny baby girl whom she called Sun.

"Because Sun was born without a father, the infant was considered a "bad-luck baby." The innocent child was labeled as a curse to the family and was marked for life. People acted in a cruel manner to this tiny baby by making faces, speaking negatively and scorning her. Right from the start of Sun's life she began to experience—and feel—rejection. Before experiencing the joy of being loved and accepted, Sun experienced the sorrow of being hated and rejected.

"Most of the people from our neighborhood were leaving, fleeing for their lives. City people came and said, 'Get out of here-quick!' With Sun on my back, our family began the six-day journey, leaving Seoul behind us. Mother had no time to rest and recuperate after Sun's birth. Without delay, we pressed our way to the south. Each of us had the responsibility of carrying the household belongings on our backs, on our heads, and in our arms. We would be so loaded down that it was hard to see our little bodies under the heavy loads of rice, clothes and blankets. At this time, my mother was thirty-two years of age; Cha was thirteen; I was ten years old; Hung Mo was eight; Oak was five; Puan was two, and little Sun was just two months old.

"Our journey to the south took place during the coldest winter I can ever remember. The severe wind felt like it would cut us to pieces. We suffered from frostbite and hunger. We saw the frozen, dead bodies of those who could not endure scattered along the way. Because of the blizzard and the tremendous amount of snow, we nearly lost our sense of direction. We were so grateful for the tracks of people who had journeyed on before us. We followed their footprints until we arrived in a little town called Mosan, Kyungido. Very few people lived there.

"This place was special; it was our father's hometown. At Mosan we began living as refugees. My mother was able to find a building where we rented a single room for the seven of us.

"Our money and food were gone. Mother and my oldest sister worked for other people in the fields. From morning until late at night they labored, leaving me to care for the four younger children. We lived on rice alone—our only food every day.

"I often carried baby Sun on my back to the fields where my mother worked. My tiny sister would be so hungry that she would cry until she was exhausted. By the time I reached mother, who desired to nurse her baby, Sun was sound asleep as a result of her incessant crying.

"Since I was responsible for the little ones in my family, I would often lead them up to the mountains. Together we would search for scraps of wood and take them to our neighbors who would give us food in exchange. Kind neighbor ladies, nursing their own babies, would volunteer to nurse Sun also. I asked many women to nurse Sun while waiting for mother to return from the fields at night.

"The people who believed in the superstition of "bad-luck babies" said that Sun cried continually because she was not believed to be a baby of blessing, but of a curse. As a result of her crying, I was not able to go to the bathroom or to sleep alone. I always carried Sun on my back as I worked, slept, and went to the bathroom. I could not let her go. She was always clinging to me. With so much rejection within her, Sun would not let me out of her sight. I became Sun's security—her rock of stability.

"Since I was so limited in what I could do with Sun on my back, my friends grew aggravated with her. They said, 'She's good for nothing.' 'You cannot do anything because of Sun.' 'Nothing good can come from her!'

Obviously, no one wanted to be around Sun. Before long I also became irritated and frustrated with my baby sister.

"During hot summer weather, with sweat running down my face, I would walk on the path in the field where my mother worked, in hopes that she would feed Sun. That would give me some relief. Again, people would spot my sister and yell, 'There goes that cry baby!' Would Sun ever grow out of her need to be constantly wailing? Would she ever become a contented child?

"Once a compassionate lady who heard Sun's annoying cry offered to nurse Sun until she quieted down.

"I began to wonder if the old superstition of the 'bad-luck baby' might be true after all.

"When the war was over, mother took Sun and my oldest sister back to Seoul to see if it was safe to return. The rest of us were left in Mosan with some relatives who were not very nice to us. They treated us like slaves. We could not even get close to them because they thought we would take advantage of them. They bossed us around by yelling and screaming at us.

"For more than two months we heard nothing from our mother. We wanted her to come and get us, but we could do nothing but wait and wonder. A day seemed like a year. The four of us wandered around crying out for mother. We would go to the top of the mountains and cry, 'Mommy! Mommy! Come get us. We want you. We miss you! Please, Mommy, come to us!' We never gave up our search for her, but it always ended in grave disappointment. What could have happened to her? Where could she be? Was she dead or alive?

"As if that were not bad enough, we also had unbelievable problems with lice. Hung Mo was hot-natured, and his infestation was worse than ours. We could actually see the lice crawling through his hair. The rest of us would gather around him and try to catch the lice and kill them.

"We grew so tired and weary as we waited for mother to return. We thought about separating from each other if mother did not return. We discussed a plan. The four of us would each go to different homes and work as slaves in order to eat and survive. In time, when we would become adults, we would meet at Ansong, a nearby city, and be together again.

"One day Hung Mo and I gathered wood and placed it together in a big bundle. He tried to place the bundle on my head, but it was too heavy and it fell into the river. In frustration, my brother and I sat on the ground and cried because our day's work had been in vain. The wood could not be retrieved. Again, we yelled for mother to come back. We were so very hungry. Now what were we to do? We had no wood to exchange for food that day. No wood, no food!

"Much to our surprise, a man appeared, seemingly out of nowhere. He helped us retrieve our bundle of wood. If he was not an angel of God, then he was surely sent from God.

"Finally, mother returned from Seoul. Because times were hard everywhere, and she was always in desperate need, she decided to give me away to a rich couple who had no children. They were to provide for me and raise me in their home and I was to work for them. It was a wonderful opportunity for me because I would want for nothing in this prosperous household; there would be food to eat, clothes to wear, a place to sleep, and money to spend!

"Despite the luxury, I could not tolerate my absence from Sun. Whatever I did, I could hear (within my mind) my brother and my sisters calling out to me. I could not sleep. I could not get them out of my mind. I was consumed with thoughts of my family. It was difficult living in plenty knowing they did not have the bare necessities.

"I had been gone less than a month when someone from Mosan approached me, and said that Sun never ceased crying—she needed me. There was an invisible bond between Sun and me which caused us to be inseparable. After thinking about the situation and the environment I was placed in, I felt compelled to leave. All I cared about was being with my family. So I returned to Mosan to be united with my loved ones. Even if we starved to death, we would at least be together.

"Mother decided to return to Seoul in hopes of uniting her family and returning to her own home to find some type of work.

"By this time, Sun was two years old. Cha, my older sister, stayed with the other children in Mosan, while mother, Sun and I started our journey back to Seoul.

"In order to reach our destination, Yongsan District in Seoul, we had to cross a bridge over the Han River. It was the only way in or out of Seoul. Much to our disdain, we learned that we had to have identification to cross the bridge. Living under dismal circumstances and in an isolated location, we did not know about this need for identification. Without the required papers, we discovered, we were considered as communists. A young boy who heard of our dilemma offered to take us across the river by boat at night. This was illegal. But we paid the boy to do this for us. We were risking a lot to cross the river—possibly our very lives!

"Since we had no money left, we sold some blankets to pay for our passage. We were ushered to a tiny, dilapidated house close to the bridge. There we saw many people without identification. These desperate people were waiting to illegally cross the river, too. We had to be extremely quiet. No one could make a noise, not even a whisper. Because the conditions were so adverse and crowded, Sun began to jabber and cry, as usual. People were frightened and greatly alarmed by her wailing. With the guards constantly patrolling the bridge close by, the people feared that the crying baby would quicken the guards to action. If they would catch us, they might do terrible things to us.

"Nothing I did pacified or silenced Sun. The other people forced us out of the tiny house because our presence placed them in jeopardy.

"The next day we returned to the house in hopes of crossing the river. Sun cried out again and we were not able to cross. It seemed we could not live with her, yet we could not live without her. What more could we do?

"In Buphung, a nearby city, we visited grandma's home. We shared our recent experiences with everyone there. They gave us unsound counsel and told us that Sun was no good and would be a constant problem to us as long as we lived. With Sun in our lives, they reminded us that we would never be successful and that she would always bring bad luck. They advised us to rid ourselves of Sun by killing her. They warned that she was a curse on our lives.

"In great frustration and anger, grandmother finally said to mother, 'Do something with that child! Get rid of her or kill her! Nothing will go right in your future, otherwise!'

"When grandmother said those hateful words, my heart was crushed and I could not bear to look at her face. I felt such contempt towards her.

"Instead of killing the child, my relatives pressured mother to rid herself of her by placing Sun in a foster home. I felt some relief because her life had been spared.

"Mother nursed Sun for one final time. With a full tummy my precious sister fell asleep. I carried her on my back and followed my aunt for a long time until we came to a big house.

"When the childless couple brought Sun inside, they gave her all kinds of candies and sweets. This kept Sun happy and occupied, since she had never had sweets before. My aunt motioned for me to leave with her, since Sun was so content.

"As we walked towards grandma's house, I kept my head down and stared at the ground. I hated my aunt so much for leaving Sun there. I could not bear to look at her.

"Without Sun on my back, it seemed as if a part of me was missing. Mother was so crushed by Sun's absence I thought her heart would break. When we returned home, she refused to eat and lay with a blanket over her head. She could not face any more heartache. She was in mourning for her baby.

"I could not stand any more inward pain either, so I decided to take a walk. Night was drawing nigh, and I walked and walked.

"Before I realized it, I came to the house where Sun was. As I came close to the window, I peeked inside by standing on my tiptoes. I even put my ear up to the window. Seeing the couple talking to Sun, and knowing I could not be with her, I sat down and cried.

"Suddenly, I felt a hand on my neck and someone sternly said, 'Get up!'

"In shock and fear, I looked up. To my disappointment, I saw my aunt standing there. 'I've looked all over town for you! I figured you'd be here,' she accused sharply.

"On the way home, my aunt continued to rebuke me, and her words wounded me deeply.

"The next day, however, I returned to the house with Sun's baby blanket. Again, I put my ear against the window. Sure enough, I could hear Sun, crying as loudly as she could. My heart sank. If only she would look at me, then I could comfort her. What was I to do? I remembered my aunt threatening me by saying, 'If you go back to Sun, you will die!' Because of Sun's reputation, mother had to stay away from her at all cost. Again I started to cry.

"The couple heard me crying and told me to get away. They were having enough trouble with Sun because all she did was cry, cry, cry. They were about to go crazy. I would just make matters worse, they reasoned.

"Just as I expected, the foster father came to grandma's home. He wanted my family to leave town because we were a threat to him and his wife. They feared that one of us would try to get Sun back.

"Mother and I went back to the Han River. We were planning to cross it again, this time without Sun. The night was pitch-dark and not a sound could be heard in the tiny house. We waited until 3:00 am to get aboard the boat.

"The man who paddled the boat said in a trembling voice, 'Please, please be careful. I want you to make it home safely.'

"Why do you say that, sir?' I asked.

"He explained, 'For several days in a row, all the people who crossed the river and reached the beach were killed by the guards!'

"The guards used search lights on the beach to look for refugees. If the people had no identification, the guards had no way to determine which Koreans were communists and which ones were not.

"If Sun had not been crying when we attempted to cross the river three days previously, death would have awaited us on the other side. Since we had been forced to leave because of Sun's crying, our lives had been spared by the grace of God. This time Sun's crying had turned out to be a blessing instead of a curse.

"With fear and anxiety deep in our hearts, we crossed the Han River. Before reaching the shore, we got out of the boat and began wading in the shallow water. To keep out of sight, we lay flat on our bellies and crawled on the sand like snakes. We were covered with sand—what a sight we were!

"Thinking we were safe, we began to walk for quite a distance. My heart nearly stopped when I heard a policeman shout, 'Stop!' We were arrested. All the while we tried to explain our situation, but he refused to believe us. He told us that we had to go back where we came from. Much to our relief, the Chief of Police granted our request to continue our journey.

"Once we reached home, mother and I began to dig up the ground and gather the dishes and belongings we had buried before our escape during the war. We sold many of our possessions so we would have some money to start our own small business. Before we were able to do this, however, the stress and strain of our circumstances had taken their toll upon mother's life. She was burdened down with so much guilt and condemnation because she gave her last baby away that she literally went blind.

" 'Come and look at me!' screamed my mother. *'I can't see!' she cried.* Mother had just awakened, and she was stricken with fear. Her eyes turned upward and only their whites could be seen. What more could happen to us? Day after day we cried in our hopeless and desperate situation. There had to be some way we could survive.

"Eventually we learned to support ourselves by selling produce in the market place. When people saw me leading my blind mother by the hand, they took notice. Out of pity, many bought our fruits and vegetables which we carried to market on our heads. Within a few months we had earned enough money to go back to Mosan and gather the rest of the children. Finally we were all back together again—except for Sun, that is.

"By the time Sun was five years old, Hung Mo was sent to grandma's house with some messages from mother. He traveled by train, but fell asleep and missed his stop. When he woke up he got off the train, but he did not know what town he was in.

"Since he was a child, the local police contacted mother. We took a train to the town where Hung Mo was waiting.

"After we picked him up, mother decided to stop at grandma's home. Mother inquired about Sun's welfare. My aunt informed her that Sun had been placed in a orphanage.

" 'Why?' asked mother, deeply concerned.

" 'Her foster parents couldn't tolerate her incessant wailing,' my aunt answered with a long sigh.

"We rushed to the foster parents' house to learn where Sun was.

"We learned that they had lied to the director of the orphanage to get rid of Sun. They said that they had found her in the street. We demanded that the foster parents should obtain a witness from the village that they had gotten Sun from my mother.

"When we had the document in hand, we all went to get my young sister. Her location was in a Catholic orphanage in the town of Inchun.

"The orphanage had given Sun a new name. She was called 'Isaiah', which means 'deliverer'.

"Rejection had always been an integral part of Sun's life. Whenever she became attached to someone, she was taken away and given to another person. She was taken away from me and her mother; her foster parents had given her away, too. Sun had learned to think that the nun who raised her at the orphanage was her mother and now, again, she was being taken away from her only security. Sun did not ever recognize us, and once again began her all-too-familiar crying.

"We made our way home with Sun on mother's back. All the while, we rejoiced and were extremely grateful to have our little Sun back so that we could be a family again. I can remember mother dancing even though she was blind.

"Soon after our reunion with Sun, mother regained her sight and has never had any problems since. She is now sixty-nine years old, and still says that the happiest day of her life was when she brought Sun home from the orphanage."

2

And Now Sun's Story

"...Choose ye this day what God ye shall serve..."
(Josh. 24:15).

When I was reunited with my family, I shared with them the things I had learned in the orphanage. I tried to teach them to fold their hands before meals and pray, "Thank you, Jesus, for this food. Thank you, Jesus, for my family. Thank you for loving me." My family ignored my instructions, and this reaction hurt me. I cried and cried because of more rejection. They continued to call me "crybaby," and the neighbors joined in with this taunting nickname.

In a short span of time I adjusted to my "new" family. With rejection deeply rooted within me, I stuck close to my mother whenever she was home.

When I was six years old, as mother was cooking a big meal, I remember sitting near the fireplace with its blazing fire under the cooking pot. I watched her cook for a while, but eventually became very drowsy from the heat. As I drifted off to sleep, my head fell against the boiling pot. The pot tipped over and the boiling water spilled out onto the fire and spattered all over me. My face was badly burned.

Mother and my sister Ann ripped their aprons off and covered me with them. They took me outside and removed the aprons. As they did so, they discovered they had made a mistake by placing them on me, because when they removed the cloth, the blistered skin came off with it! My face was a terrible mess and huge blisters formed all over my deep red skin. They rushed me to the hospital where the doctors covered my head with bandages. I looked like a mummy with only my eyes, nose, and mouth showing.

Remembering my history, people made comments like, "It would have been better if Sun had never left the orphanage."

"She could have been spared this horrible tragedy if you would have left her at the orphanage."

"She'll be scarred for life."

"Her face can't possibly recover from this."

"She will be an ugly sight."

I was the "bad-luck child." Wherever I was, it always seemed there was a problem to encounter.

The day my bandages were removed, however, my facial skin was like a baby's. It was a miracle; God was trying to reveal Himself to my Buddhist family.

As I grew up, my mother was always desperately looking for work. She began to sell liquor in front of our home, but the liquor business turned out to be a real mess.

The drunks would vomit and relieve themselves in our yard and in the neighbors' yards, as well. Because drunkards tend to be uninhibited, they felt no shame, and showed no modesty. The rank smell caused by their behavior was so horrendous that I became nauseous. The compelling lust for alcohol overpowered the men. They charged their drink and came back for more. When mother confronted them for payment, they would push her around and continue to take advantage of her.

Frustrated with their wanton behavior, mother sat on the ground with her legs stretched out in front of her, beating her chest and blatantly blaming her dead husband for all the troubles and woes she had had to endure.

Lost in her pity party, she cried out,"Why did you give all these children and then leave me? I cannot take any more of this suffering."

At the lowest ebb of her life, many times mother tried to commit suicide. Once, we had to prevent her from stabbing herself. Another time, as the family was sleeping, someone heard a strange noise; it was the sound of mother trying to choke herself with a rope around her neck.

These dreadful sights and memories caused the already deep feelings of insecurity and rejection to continue to root deeper within the inner recesses of my being.

In great desperation, I would frequently cry, "Mommy! Mommy! Please don't cry. When I grow up, I will take care of you and make lots of money for you so the drunkards will not treat you bad any more!"

Day after day, I tried to comfort her, but my efforts were in vain.

As I developed into young womanhood, I grew hateful and bitter. I began to question my miserable lot in life. Why did I have to live in such adverse conditions: with hurt, poverty, rejection, loneliness, and without a father? I lacked so much!

I resented the fact that I always had to wear "hand-me-downs." With four older sisters, those clothes had gone through a lot of wear and tear by the time I got them.

I soon became obsessed with the love of money. My mind was consumed with thoughts of earning money. Nothing could hold back this inner drive that surged within me.

In Korea, the government does not provide public education after the sixth grade. Mother had no money for us to go further in school. That did not stop me, however. Being a persistent person with a stubborn nature, I was determined to work my way through school, even if it meant going to night school.

After I graduated from grammar school, I learned of an American missionary school which provided classes for students in seventh, eighth and ninth grades. In order to attend, I had to make monthly payments. Since mother was unable to support me, I took on an illegal sales job. I felt I had to accept this job, because if I did not get an education, I would not be able to get a good job. Without a good job, I reasoned, there would be no money in my pocket. If I had no money in my pocket, I would be better off dead. I was sick and tired of this miserable life I was in... .

There were coffee shops in our country which sold drinks like coffee and tea. My sales job took business away from these coffee shops because I would walk from one company to another and serve hot tea. Because of my service, workers did not have to leave their place of employment to purchase their beverages. They greatly appreciated this convenience.

The coffee shop owners, of course, felt differently about the work I did. One day I was reprimanded by some of them. They threatened me by saying, "Who do you think you are selling your illegal tea in our territory?" They then continued their threats by saying they would make things very hard for me and the owners I worked for by reporting us to the police. I was frightened by them and felt such humiliation over what they were saying to me in this public place that I could feel the old roots of hate and rejection growing deeper in the soil of my heart.

Another embarrassing experience occurred one time as I rode with my tea on a bus packed with people. When the bus jolted, the hot tea from my thermos splashed on a passenger's leg. She shrieked at me in a loud voice, "What is this?!!"

This incident tore me up inside, and matters worsened when a lady who was taking the bus fare forbade me to enter the bus. She pushed me away in front of the onlookers. I had to walk to my destinations in the bitterly cold weather. In spite of my seeming success, these events caused me to lose all my self-esteem and confidence.

Even at home, when family or friends would gather, the "bad-luck baby's" story of rejection was a favorite topic of discussion. Would I always be an object of ridicule?

I wondered what my purpose for living was. Why was I here? Who am I? I might as well be dead. Somehow, I would manage to get hold of myself and remind myself that I could finish school, get a job and one day get rich.

In the American missionary school, we were required to attend Wednesday night church meetings. Nothing in these services had a positive effect on me. I was bored in the meetings and felt they were a waste of time. Sometimes I even slept through the sermons; other times, I would use the time to figure the profits from my tea sales. I attended only because I had to.

The missionaries taught against witchcraft and fortune tellers, and told us we could not serve Buddha, and that we ought not to drink liquor or smoke. Well, my mother was involved with most of the areas they taught against: she sold liquor, served Buddha, and visited fortune tellers. Mother refused to allow me to serve the American God. Since she was a devoted Buddhist, she wanted nothing to do with Christians because she thought they would bring bad luck. Mother's heart was so hardened.

One Wednesday night when I was in the eighth grade, as the preacher talked about heaven and hell, I opened myself up to the fear of death. I was so burdened and weighed down with thoughts of death because I had no security; I was neither Buddhist nor Christian. I was not prepared to die. I was in a living hell and at the same time I knew if I died I would be in an eternal hell. Could the second hell be any worse than the one I was living in?

After two years of Wednesday night church meetings, the Holy Spirit began to melt the hardness of my heart. Still I would not surrender my life to God. At that time, I saw a lot of Christian people living in poverty. I was afraid that if I became a Christian I would never be rich.

In my heart I fought with the Holy Spirit. I wanted to be in control of my life! I wanted to be the boss! I would be rich! I would make myself a success! I would show everybody! No one would be able to put me down any more! I would see to that! With defiant thoughts in my mind, I knew that all I needed was just a little more time to prove myself. *My dreams would come true!* They just had to....

As the preacher continued to share about the love of the Lord and how He gave His life for us, I resisted the message and tried to tune it out. But the thought persisted; Somebody died for me? You have to be kidding! Was this the truth or a lie?

I had pretended to be a Christian at school and was too proud to reveal the truth and risk rejection again.

My heart kept pounding. Finally, I didn't care about anything or anyone. Something happened! Out of the fear of hell, I found myself going to the front of the chapel. At last I would be assured of heaven. The preacher asked if I wanted to receive Jesus into my heart. I answered, "Yes!" After prayer I was baptized in water.

A few weeks later, after night school, some girl friends and I spent all night praying and singing in the chapel. When I returned home early the next morning, filled with the excitement of God's presence in my life, my mother was waiting, having worried all night. "Where was Sun? Is she alright?"

I bubbled over with excitement. I couldn't wait to share with my family what had happened to me. Mother listened and then exploded with great anger by telling me, "We cannot serve two gods in one family! The American God will bring bad luck to our family. The two gods will fight, resulting in more poverty, sickness and trouble. For generations our family has served Buddha, and *you will serve Buddha too!*"

My mother's constant insistence that our family must not be divided in our service to Buddha brought confusion to my mind.

I continued to carry contempt and rebellion in my heart because I did not fully understand salvation. I was living a phony life. People thought I was happy and content, but I fooled them—I was still miserable. It did not take long before I fell away, and put the whole experience behind me.

Again I determined in my heart, "No matter the price to be paid, I will be rich." Nothing would stand in my way! I had made my choice. Money would be my god.

3

A Way Out

In Korea we had a tradition of esteeming men higher than women. The men were treated like kings. The women remained subservient to men and were not even allowed to eat in the same room with a man. When a male child was born, the family celebrated and rejoiced, but not so with the birth of a female child. The son was of great importance.

As the only son, my brother would become the leader of our household. Hung Mo would be responsible for supporting and providing for each family member under the same roof, and would be the one who would carry on the family name.

Korean men are required to join the army for three years. So, at the early age of nineteen, Hung Mo joined the army. He wanted to complete his obligation to his country so he could return home to mother, who remained in great financial need.

One day, much to our surprise, we opened the front door to find Hung Mo leaning on crutches. He appeared so thin and looked terrible. He explained that he had had surgery on his back. Because of his disability, he was discharged from the army a year early. The reason he had not informed us of his setback was that he did not want to put any more burdens on mother.

As Hung Mo's health grew worse and worse, mother called for the help of a woman who practiced witchcraft. Mother believed that this woman's incantations and spells and rituals would alter my brother's condition. The woman came to our home and said, "There are many spirits harassing your family. A curse has been put on your son because your dead husband's spirit can find no rest and peace, so he is just roaming around until he can find rest. You will have to appease the spirits in order to send them away to find their resting place. We will have a big celebration."

We did as she recommended, and during the celebration this eerie woman spoke with the exact sound of my father's voice and the voices of many others who had passed away. I heard this voice saying, "Do you want me to bless you or do you want me to destroy you?" As my mother rubbed her hands the bowing up and down, which is the customary action of a person who is asking for forgiveness. The spirit went on to say, "I want you to make my heart so that I can find rest and leave you alone." My mother was so fearful by this time that all she could do was continually bow down and plead with the spirit to bless us and she promised to give the spirit whatever he desired to make him happy so that he could find rest and leave us alone. I wondered, how in the world can a man's voice come out of a woman's body? It was all very frightening. It was as though someone or some power took over her body. Was that possible? I was beginning to believe it was... .

This strange woman reassured us that as soon as the spirits found rest, Hung Mo would recover.

During this celebration, all our family members and many neighbors watched as someone beat a drum with a constant, steady rhythm. Others danced and some cried. This spooky woman actually walked on the blade of a huge, sharp knife. She even carried a hundred-pound pig on her shoulders. I never would have believed it if I had not seen it. Not one mark was left on the bottom of her feet.

There was a table filled with all of the food we had all so many times desired and hungered for. There was all different kinds of rice cakes and cookies, korean pancakes, all types of vegetables, many fish and a very large cooked pig's head. The food was placed there for the spirits to eat and be pacified; afterwards the spirits would leave us alone. People bowed and worshipped in front of the food in honor of the spirits.

It was all a great expense for mother. The celebration had to be repeated many times, but she was willing to pay the price. Mother was determined to see that her only son was healed, so she worked long, hard hours to pay for it all. She was working when I got up in the morning and she was working when I went to bed at night.

Mother also begged Buddha to intervene, but nothing she tried helped Hung Mo. Even when mother served rice to Buddha, and presented him with money, there was no improvement. Even though Buddha was no help, mother remained a loyal servant to her pagan god.

With no insurance or money left, mother had to resort to selling the only thing we had left — the house. This would enable Hung Mo to have a second operation. But the second surgery did not help either.

At age twenty-two, Hung Mo was not able to carry his load of responsibility. Instead of his supporting the family, mother had to continue to support us. Hung Mo was gravely disappointed and deeply frustrated, and he vented his pent-up emotions by frequently yelling at us.

With so much strife and contention in our home, I found myself occupying my time elsewhere, by going to parties and spending time with friends at dances. These activities enabled me to forget my self-pitying thoughts of my sorry life. I became the life of the party. "Let's invite Sun!" my friends would say; "She's a blast!"

When Hung Mo found out that I was out socializing with my friends, he felt hurt and angry because he could not go out and have fun. His dreams of marriage and a fulfilling future were dashed to pieces. Since he could not go out and have fun, he did not want me to, either.

He grew worse with each passing day and became more antagonistic. I consistently lied to him in order to escape his presence. I lied to him, "I am going to baby-sit for a teacher." Or, I would say something like, "My friend's father is dying, so I must go and comfort her."

Then I would leave the house to be with my friends who helped me forget my problems, and even myself.

When my brother learned of my deceptive schemes and caught on to my whereabouts, he began to beat me.

He would take a belt or a switch and abuse me. He resented my freedom.

By the time I was a sophomore in high school, two of my sisters had gotten married. This left my mother, my brother, and two other sisters. The five of us moved to the village of Samkacge, also in the District of Yongsan Seoul. It was located close to a U.S. Army station. Everywhere we looked, we could see an American.

We lived in an open market where mother cooked and served food. She was an excellent cook. She prepared Korean sausage and Korean pancakes. Koreans and Americans came from all over to eat mother's delicacies.

Behind our place of business, the five of us lived in a single room.

During my teenage years, Hung Mo and mother refused to allow me to date a man who was seven years older than me. Mother planned to choose my future mate like she had done for my two sisters. They felt I was foolish to get so involved in this relationship. Besides, they considered him much too old for me.

I refused to be matched up and married to a man I did not want. I planned to make my own choice. We thought we were in love and planned for the future. He sacrificed to buy me things and tried to please me. After dating for four years I decided to break off our relationship, not because Hung Mo told me to, but because my love of money outweighed my love for the man. He was from a poor family like mine.

My husband would have to be prosperous. Otherwise, I would remain single. It did not matter to me whether the man was crippled, a widower, or old — just so he was wealthy. My rebellion deepened against Hung Mo and mother. I was determined to rule my own life.

I continued working my way through school. During my senior year in high school I got a job as a custodian in a Korean bank. Each day my responsibility involved the cleaning of a huge office. Also, I acted as a "gopher." Whenever the workers needed supplies, I gathered the items needed and delivered them.

I continued working in the bank after graduation. One evening after work, I decided not to return home because I was so weary of the depressing atmosphere and the continual contention with Hung Mo. Instead, I attended a social activity. Little did I know what was awaiting me when I got home — a horrible beating! Hung Mo beat me with a rubber hose so hard that I nearly passed out. I begged him to stop, but he was furious with me for coming home so late at night. I was terribly exhausted from all the abuse and noticed unsightly marks across my back from the hose. I could never allow myself to talk back to Hung Mo because I feared he might kill me.

One day during the summer of 1969, as I was chatting with some classmates, one of the girls mentioned a way to make some good money. Immediately she had my attention because I deceived myself into believing that money would solve all my problems. Since I was not making much money at the bank, I became interested in this new opportunity. The wheels of my mind were turning, but I tried to appear uninterested.

The job description sounded decent enough. Only females were hired. They were like personal waitresses who wait on high-class people: politicians, businessmen, doctors, bankers and lawyers. The women's responsibilities were to serve the men food and drinks, to listen to them, and to be friendly. Also, they had to be able to dance and to carry on an intelligent conversation because these were highly educated men. I felt I could handle a job like that, so I called the employment agency my friends talked about. A man answered the phone and told me to meet him at a particular coffee shop at a specific time. There was much secrecy because this line of work was connected with an illegal private club. The man who met with me wanted to scrutinize me personally in order to see how attractive I was, and to find out whether or not I was involved with the police. The men took no risks. Security measures were of utmost priority.

Since this business was illegal, the man led me to an ordinary-looking home where I was hired. The location had to remain inconspicuous. As I returned I saw many rooms. In one room there were a number of women putting on make-up, getting dressed the traditional Korean attire, and preparing themselves for work. They were beautiful.

The owner of the house was a woman. She began to inquire about my qualifications. "Can you sing? Can you dance? Are you friendly with people? These things are important as a hostess. You will be dealing with important men."

Normally the women who could lure and attract men were hired. The type of women who had the ability to draw the men back for more food and entertainment were the ones who were most in demand.

When the owner accepted me, my heart pounded like a drum. It was a big step for me, especially in such a risky business. I committed myself to another illegal job. Unknown to me, I was walking into a trap; but all I cared about was making money.

On the way home, I had to figure out what to tell Hung Mo and my mother. I decided to tell them I had been hired by a former teacher of mine to help him with a night class. When I explained this to them, they gave me permission to work the night job. After all, we needed the money.

When I went to work the first evening, some ladies asked, "Why do you want to work in this kind of place? You are so innocent-looking. You better get out, right now, if you can!"

My face blushed with embarrassment, as they told me this. Personally, I saw no harm with this occupation. What could be so bad about serving men? These women went on with comments that caused me to question my decision. But the burning desire to be rich calmed all my doubts.

With great anticipation, I observed the behavior and the manners of the other ladies as they worked with the men. They carried themselves graciously and with great charm and confidence. They treated the men royally.

Fearful thoughts entered my mind. What if I do not please the men? What if one refuses me and requests another woman to replace me? Can I deal with more rejection? I wanted so much to perform well.

Much to my surprise, the night was a success. I was a good hostess and got along very well with the men I served. I was especially pleased with the money I made in the one night. It was very late. All I could think about as I hurried home was the money I would make the next night.

The next day, I worked at the Korean bank, and then went back to the private club that evening. I noticed a fine-looking customer enter the club. I learned his name was Lee. Lee had a very handsome fellow with him named Kim. I was taken aback by their friendliness and courtesy. They recognized I was a new girl at the club because I was ill-at-ease and a bit awkward. After we all sat down, I served them liquor and visited with them.

When I left the club that night I could not locate a bus or a taxi because it was very close to time for curfew. No traffic, nor pedestrians, were allowed on the streets past midnight. My heart was full of anxiety, because I did not know what to do. Kim had left earlier in the evening. When Lee saw my predicament, he offered to have his driver take me home. I consented. I was impressed. I thought this businessman must have been loaded with money because he had his own car. Only the rich could afford cars in Korea, and the rich hired their own drivers. With excitement, I jumped into his car.

With a cool voice Lee said, "Since it is so close to curfew it will take too long to go the thirty miles to your home. We could all be arrested, so let's stay in a motel for the night." I definitely did not like that idea, but in the situation I did not have much of a choice. I could not get home, but I did not want to be arrested.

I was naive and felt that Lee and his driver were trustworthy, so I agreed to stay in a motel for the night. I could not sleep, so I just laid there. Then, all of a sudden, Lee jumped on me. I wanted to scream, but he put his hand over my mouth. I tried to push him away, but he overpowered me. After Lee had finished raping me, I felt so dirty and ashamed.

In Korea, when a woman lost her virginity, she was considered an outcast. Decent men wanted nothing to do with her; she was marked as a dirty, base woman. Most men lost all respect for her. When a husband and wife consummated their marriage and the man doubted her virginity, he would be furious. There were instances where the marriage was broken because the wife had not saved herself for her husband.

The next morning, I went home feeling so disgusted and ashamed. As I entered the house, I tried to avoid a confrontation with Hung Mo and mother.

As soon as Hung Mo saw me, he said, "I do not want you to go to work today. I want to talk to you. But first, I want you to sit in the corner. You are to say nothing and do nothing!"

As the leader of our family, Hung Mo was responsible for me. I took advantage of his headship and did not respect him. I resented his severe punishment, but I said "OK!"

Since Hung Mo had spent the night worrying about me and being a sick man, he was exhausted. He told me to stay in the corner while he slept for a while, and then he would talk to me. I did not trust Hung Mo because many times he had threatened to do terrible things to me like breaking my leg or shaving my head. Shaving one's head was a sign of humiliation.

Sitting in the corner, I was scared to death. I knew Hung Mo had had enough of my lies and deceitful schemes. He would not put up with much more. He would be waiting to teach me another lesson with severe punishment.

As I sat there thinking these dreadful thoughts, I could not figure out why mother and Hung Mo found it so difficult to understand me. I wanted to be rich in order to provide for them and make life easier for all of us. I thought they must be sick and tired of being poor. What was wrong with them? I felt I was doing them a favor by trying to support myself.

Then I remembered Lee's words to me the night before, "Why are you working here? I hate seeing you working in a joint like this. You are so young and innocent. If there is anything I can do to help you get out of this place, I will do it. So here is my phone number. Feel free to call me if I can be of any help."

Even though I had experienced such horrible degradation from him the previous night, Lee's offer gave me a ray of hope. I picked up a few belongings while Hung Mo was sleeping and sneaked out of the house.

I took a bus to downtown Seoul. As soon as I sat down I began to cry. What was to happen to me if Lee refused to help? Leaving home was a serious matter. My heart pounded with fear and worry. "What will happen to mother when she discovers I'm gone?" Through my tears, I promised mother I would come home again when I had enough money to take care of her.

The crowded bus arrived in the downtown section of Seoul. I got off and went to a nearby coffee shop. I took Lee's phone number from my purse and gave him a call.

Great hope was in my heart. "Lee," I said. "I ran away from home this morning and I need your help."

Much to my disappointment, he did not sound the same as he had the night before. There was coldness in his voice and he gave me various excuses why he could not meet me then. He reassured me that he would meet me at the club later that evening.

After I hung up, my mind was flooded with depressing thoughts. There was no way I could return home; I would not even consider it. Hung Mo would make life worse than ever. My future looked so dark and gloomy. I did not have the slightest idea where my life was headed. I had come this far and there was no turning back.

I thought about calling my friends, but I didn't think they would understand. With nowhere to go and no one to talk to, I sat in the coffee shop the rest of the day.

4

The Man of My Dreams

That night I went back to work at the club. Lee and Kim returned to the club. Lee stopped by to talk to me privately, as he had promised. I told him that I had no place to stay.

"Where am I going to go? I don't have enough money to rent a place. Can you help me?" I asked desperately. Lee talked to the club owner, who offered me a place to stay temporarily. I was a little hesitant to accept this offer, because I did not want the owner to take advantage of me and force me to do anything immoral against my will. Much to my relief, Lee informed the owner of my concerns, and the owner promised to respect my wishes.

That night, as I wallowed in great self-pity, I drank myself into intoxication. Uninhibited, I danced like a wild woman. I really let go! I lured the men with my lewd movements.

As the evening wore on, Lee's buddy, Kim, took particular notice of me. He was a thirty-two-year-old bachelor. He walked up to me and said, "Wow! you are quite a dancer! You sure turn me on!" I was so drunk and was feeling so depressed that nothing mattered to me.

I replied, "Who cares?"

He continued, "I want to talk with you alone, but Lee never gives us a chance to be alone."

The days went by and one night two weeks later Kim and Lee came to drink and see me. I thought their attention was sweet, but as usual Lee would not let me out of his sight. Finally he had to leave the room. While he was gone Kim saw his chance to talk to me alone. Then he walked over to a corner and he told me that Lee was a married man with three children. I asked, "Why are you telling me this?"

He answered, "I do not think you are aware of this dangerous game you are playing. He can never marry you. Why let him hurt you?"

"I am not planning to marry Lee. Besides, he has been good to me by helping me find a place to live."

"Granted he is a good man, but you need to let him be free. By the way, you are not aware of how badly Lee feels since he hurt you the other night. The only reason he has been coming to see you is out of guilt. He has too many obligations right now, and his wife is starting to notice that something is wrong with him. They are having a lot of marital problems. I think it is time to let him go."

He continued, "I am single and available. Here's my number if you are interested. I am very interested in seeing you." Since I had no feelings of love for Lee and I had no desire to break up a marriage and hurt three children, I decided to let Lee go. After all, Kim was a man without obligation.

Kim did not mince words with me. He was aggressive and bold — and I found these qualities very appealing. He was full of wonderful qualities: he was compassionate; muscular; well-educated; suave; handsome; and most importantly, he was wealthy.

He swept me off my feet, and I trusted my life to him. I swallowed his line, for I was so naive and infatuated with him. He seemed to have his life "all together" — the man of my dreams. As soon as our conversation was over, Lee entered the room. He said it was time to go. As he left I followed, telling him what I knew and that I would not make any trouble for him. I assured him I would be alright. Lee was greatly relieved that I understood. The next day Kim and I met at a coffee shop to talk. He made me a proposition I found hard to refuse.

He said, "You know, I have been involved in a business with a lot of pressure and headaches. My father gave me quite a bit of money to start this business. Also, I have loaned a lot of money to other people who have not repaid me. I have been under so much stress, I would love to get away from here and rest.

"It sounds like you need the same thing, too. Maybe we could go to a beach and relax. I have been with a lot of girls, but there is something different about you that attracts me. You are so sincere and easy to love. Hey, kid, what do you say? Let's find a nice place and spend some time together."

My heart was pounding.

He added, "We do not have to sleep together. Just being with you is all I care about, so don't be scared. If you are willing to make love, fine. If not, then that is fine, too. I am not going to force you into anything. I just want to be with you."

Kim told me that if I chose to accompany him, then I would have to give up my job at the club. I had only been working there for two weeks, but Kim had greater priority in my life than the job did. I thought Kim had more money than I knew what to do with. At nineteen years of age, I thought I would be set for life. I accepted his invitation and, before I realized it, I was falling in love. Somehow, I wanted to make him a part of my life.

Kim dropped me off at a motel and promised to return with his suitcase. Later that night he returned, but without the suitcase. "My family had a lot of company at the house," he said. "With all the confusion, I left without my suitcase. Tomorrow I will go home and pack and we will leave."

The following day he returned. Again I noticed he did not have the suitcase with him. Instead he had some liquor in his hands. As he saw the surprised look on my face, he began drinking and said, "Hey, kid, we need to talk." Gently, he put his hand on my shoulder and put his forehead on my forehead then continued, "I have fallen in love with you. I have never met a more unique woman. I really appreciate how you sacrificed your job for me. I realize you were bringing in good tips. But, I love you too much to see you working there. Someone owes me quite a bit of money, and I promise you that I will get it today, then we will spend a week's vacation together."

My heart melted like butter, as I swallowed his every word. Kim kissed me tenderly on the lips. He knew just what to do and say. He had a way of making me want him.

In my heart, I knew I had him, and I was planning to keep him. Whatever it took, I was willing to do anything to please him. I gave myself completely over to him. It was wonderful to be loved and accepted. I felt I had been denied love through the years. Kim understood me like no one else had ever done.

Kim returned the next day, but this time he was drunk and he came without the suitcase again. But he treated me like a somebody. I felt like I was in a fantasy world.

Sun in 1967 at age 17.

Just before I met Kim—
age 19

5

My Dream Became a Nightmare

Two months passed. Kim and I had not taken that vacation yet. Nonetheless he remained faithful in coming to see me daily, and taking care of the motel bills and meals for me. I wondered why he kept delaying the trip, but I patiently waited.

One day, Kim's mother came to see me at the motel. She asked, "So you know what has been going on? Do you know what he has been doing? We cannot keep anything in our home. He stole the stereo which he sold to pay for your motel room. He also stole the radio and some jewelry until we caught on to him."

"Oh, my goodness!" I thought. "I am involved with a dangerous, desperate man and he has no money of his own." My heart sank.

His mother went on, "I think you need to leave my son alone, and to go back to your house to be with your family."

"I cannot go back to my home, but I will do something about it," I replied. After she left, fear and loneliness overwhelmed me. What was I going to do? I could not go back to my home, and I had no money to stay here.

That afternoon Kim came to the motel. I could see he was drunk again. He came very close to me and said, "I need to tell you a few things. For one thing, I cannot pay the motel bill any longer and I do not love you. You are going to have to go home. I *will not* and *cannot* be responsible for you. The only reason I took care of you the past couple of months was out of pity. When I saw you at the club, you were like a little girl who was lost in a big world. I was disturbed to see you involved at that club, because it does not take much time before the girls become hookers. I hated to see you get into that racket. You are too good for that."

By then, I realized Kim had merely used me. My dream turned into a nightmare. I regretted what I had gotten myself into, but it was too late to do anything about it. I hated myself for being used by a man. I wanted to hide; I felt so low. I felt more rejection and felt there was only a dead end for me. Where could I go? What could I do? During this period of deep confusion and depression, I noticed a change taking place in my body. I was unusually sleepy and was suffering morning sickness, as well as having menses.

A medical examination disclosed that I was pregnant. I now had new hope because I just knew this would change Kim's mind and he would marry me.

Kim dropped by to see me once again. I could see he was drunk as usual. "Kim," I began, "there is something you need to know." I paused as he looked at me curiously. "I had an examination at the hospital, and I am pregnant. The baby is yours."

Kim became furious with me and started to slap me around and push me down. He yelled, "You are not pregnant. If you are, the baby is not mine! I just know it is not mine!" Kim was afraid of the truth. His life was already a mess and he did not want a child to compound his problems. In his heart, Kim knew he could not walk away from his own flesh and blood. This baby was just as much his as it was mine. To bear more responsibility was too much for Kim to accept at that time. He called me horrible names and kept beating me. I could not escape him.

After a night or two of leaving me alone, Kim came back to see me. He had been drinking. This time he brought a friend with him. He introduced us and we talked for a while. Then the nightmare started. To my surprise, Kim asked me to undress and make love with him in front of his friend. When I refused to do what he asked, he started beating me and forced me to make love anyway.

Afterwards, I felt horrified and humiliated. I struck back at him by trying to hide in different places in the motel, but he always found me. Finally, I just took off running out the door and down the street. Being angry at Kim and myself for what had happened, and because of my fear of him and all the other confusion, I did not care what would happen to me. While I was running like a wild animal, a policeman stopped me. It was after midnight curfew. Kim was in close pursuit behind me.

On the way to the police station, the officer asked me who this man was, and I told the policeman that Kim was my fiance, and that we had had an argument. Kim told the policeman that I was not his fiance but that I was just a prostitute. We had to stay in the police station that night. Again, in front of everyone, Kim verbally abused me by shouting, "Get out of my life; I never want to see you again! You have caused me nothing but bad luck ever since we met!" It deeply hurt me to hear the same words again. Was I the "bad-luck baby" after all?

In the early morning hours they took us to the jail to wait to see the judge. In the meantime, Kim's parents came and posted bail for us both. Upon getting ready to leave, Kim told me to hurry and get out when they called my name, because he did not want his family to see me.

After my release, having no money, I had to walk ten miles back to the motel. I must have been a pretty sight to behold with no shoes on and after a sleepless night. I did not care about these things, though, as all I could do was recall, in horror, all the events of the night before. By the time I arrived at the motel I was convinced that my relationship with Kim was over.

I knew I had to start searching for a way out of all this so I could start living again. To my surprise, Kim came to see me that night. He had been in a gang fight and was bleeding. I tried to help him. He showed compassion for me by telling me he did not want to let me go unless I was going home. He said he did not want me to get lost in this big world. Before he finished telling me this, his brother, after learning about the gang fight, came and got him.

All of this, and what Kim told me, left me thinking that he really did care for me and that he loved me. Since I could not get home in my present condition all I knew was that I needed to be patient.

For a few days, Kim thought about the situation and decided to leave me for good. After he informed his parents of his decision, they were quite pleased. He requested a large sum of money from his parents to start his own business.

Kim's parents were willing to assist him in getting a small business started. In time it would grow and prosper. Getting me out of his life allowed Kim to have his parents' full financial support. It was not proper for a high-class Korean to marry a low-class Korean. People were expected to remain in their own class. For me to marry Kim would have been disgraceful for him and his family. If Kim were to marry me, it would have been likely for his parents to disinherit him.

Kim insisted that I return to my home. I cried and begged him not to force me to do this. "There is no way I can go back to my family. I will do anything! Please keep me. My brother will kill me. I would rather die here than face him!" I pled.

Kim was willing to give me money from the allotted sum for his business. He knew I was in desperate need. At that moment, I came to the realization that money did not matter to me. I loved Kim with all my heart, even though he abused me. I wanted him, I needed him.

When he was sober, Kim would show love and compassion to me. We had had some great times together. When he was so sweet and loving I was willing to die for him. But when Kim became brutal like a wild animal, I hated him and I wanted to run away and hide. I said, "I want YOU, not your money! Please let me stay with you!" Kim gave in to my pleading, so we ended up renting a very small, one-room apartment.

It was big enough for one bed and a tiny stove. There was no space for other furniture. Knowing that we were financially strapped and that a baby was on the way, Kim gave me a small amount of money for a couple of sleeping bags and a few dishes.

In a way I was glad I was pregnant. Otherwise, I would have had to return home. Being with Kim, even in a tiny room, was all that mattered to me. Living in a big, beautiful mansion with money did not matter to me any more. I totally committed myself to this man and tried to make him happy.

Kim used the money for the business in order to finance his gambling sprees and after a few months the money was completely depleted. He continued drinking a great deal, too. Having lost his money in gambling and drinking, Kim began stealing from his family again. Also, he would go to neighboring stores and charge great quantities of whiskey. Often, when he drank, he would command me to undress and dance and entertain him as he was lying on the bed. Since I always desired to please him, I obeyed. By turning him on in this manner I was able to keep him from abusing me during his drunken stupors.

I was five months pregnant, but I had no maternity clothes or food. Kim's parents refused to give him additional money, and he had no job, so I tried to make do with my regular clothes. Each day I would hope that Kim would bring some money and food home, but instead he always returned drunk. I would go all day without food — even two or three days. He neglected my needs, but continued to feed his lusts.

He would berate me by saying, "Why don't you go home? I hate you! Look what a mess you have gotten me into. Before I met you my life was great. Ever since you came, there have only been problems, and now my life is destroyed! You bring me *bad luck*..."

I winced inside as I heard those two words again - "bad luck." I tuned out the rest of his words. Would I ever be free of that curse on my life? No matter where I went, I had this terrible effect on people — I was "bad luck."

I felt that I was a tramp and I believed I was the only one to blame for Kim's failures. Maybe he would have been a success without me in his life, I reflected in shame and guilt.

Mama Lee in 1982 after
healing from stroke.

Left to Right: Sun, Mama Lee,
Sister Ann, Sister Ock—Christmas 1986

6

Hell On Earth

One day when Kim was gone, I cried out, "God are you real? What am I here for? Do I really bring bad luck? Am I to blame for all the problems?" I was so lonely and scared.

Another day I was so hungry. I spotted a bakery with all kinds of fresh-smelling, luscious baked bread. I was so tempted to steal. "How much does the bread cost?" I asked. After the owner told me, I knew I could not afford it. So, I asked a neighbor how I could make a little money in order to buy some bread. She suggested that I carry water for people.

Some people had no running water in their homes, so they had to purchase it, bringing their own containers to a certain place, filling them with water, and then carrying them back to their homes. Some did not want to carry the heavy containers of water, and they were willing to pay someone to do it for them.

I was five months pregnant, famished, and penniless. But I was willing to do the task. I placed a pole over my shoulders; on each side of the pole I carried five gallons of water. The load was so heavy and I was weak from hunger. I thought I was going to pass out. "God, help me!" I cried under my burdens — the burden on my shoulders and the one within my heart.

My intense hunger motivated me to continue this heavy work. One day Kim came home with some rice. I asked him where he got it. "Don't worry about it, just eat," he replied. I was so thrilled to have food. After I prepared it, I ate and ate and ate. I could not stop eating.

On another day, he brought home some kimchee — a Korean vegetable dish that is eaten with rice. I asked Kim where he got it, and he gave me the same reply.

"This may come as a shock to you, but I found out that I am sterile. That baby you are carrying isn't mine; it belongs to Lee. Believe me, the doctor informed me of my condition," Kim explained.

I tried to prove to Kim that the child was his, not Lee's. I could prove it by the dates, but he still denied his capability to impregnate.

It dazed me when he said, "When you have this baby, I can adopt the child. You will be free to go your way, and I will marry someone who will raise the baby."

"What? No! We are going to raise this baby together!" I shouted.

"No, kid, I told you *no*"

Each time I reminded Kim that it was his baby, he slapped me. "How else can I prove it to you, Kim?"

He responded, "Let me tell you something, kid! With your reputation at the private club, there is no way I will allow you to shame my family! My family's name is honorable and you aren't going to pollute it!"

His harsh words pierced my heart. Kim continued, "We are in two different classes. My family will not accept you. Low class and high class just don't mix. Besides, I don't even love you. You only used me because you thought I was a rich man."

At first, I had wanted his money, but as I fell in love with him, the money meant nothing. I tried to prove that to him, but it was no use. As if he had not wounded and rejected me enough, Kim complained, "Besides, I want a woman who is pure and respectful. Your first time wasn't with me!"

Each day grew darker and more hopeless. I was at my wit's end. I felt so worthless. I had hurt my family. My friends were successful — I was dirt. All my hopes and dreams had backfired. Even as I walked in the midst of people, I felt like an outcast and thought others pointed at me. I was beyond tears. I could not even cry any more. I was so worn out with my filthy living.

I thought of my mother working in the restaurant. Surely I would not starve if I went home. At least I would have food to eat. But then I remembered what Hung Mo would do to me, and how I would shame them by returning. I realized I would rather die than face them. My life had fallen apart.

Full of guilt and self-hatred, I grew deeper and deeper into depression. I strongly considered suicide. I could not bear the reality of my child coming into this world without a father — another "bad-luck baby." Could I not do anything right? I was tormented with the thoughts of conceiving a "bad-luck baby." Before my child's birth, I felt responsible for labeling its precious life. If I died, I reasoned, the baby would also die and escape the kind of life I had lived.

For some unknown reason, Kim could not totally break free of me. He took notice of my changed behavior. I obviously was not well, emotionally or physically. He softened his attitude towards me. I never wanted to upset Kim because I feared losing him, so I did not bother to tell him when I ran out of rice. When he was hungry, he went to his mother's to eat.

I grew weaker and weaker each day. With the combination of depression and hunger, I became physically ill. I could hardly get out of bed. When Kim saw that the rice container was empty, he felt awful. He began to steal rice and kimchee from his mother's storehouse. There was enough rice to last for a year. There was enough kimchee to last through the winter months for the whole family. There was so much food that no one noticed it was missing.

With a tear running down his face, Kim said, "Hey, kid, you need to eat. I want you to be strong. I want you to make it." Knowing where the food came from, I could not eat it. Kim took great pains to get it for me, but I refused it.

We both began to cry and he confessed that he truly loved me, but he could not marry me because of the difference in our social classes. With tears in his eyes he said, "I am no good to you. You can do better than me. I may come from a rich home, but I have nothing worthwhile to offer you. If you married me, you would regret it for the rest of your life."

He really does care for me, I thought. I never expected the advice he gave to me in the next breath, "Why don't you consider aborting the baby or giving it away?"

He was serious! I was shocked with disbelief. How could he suggest such a thing? During times of depression, I toyed with the idea, but I did not think I could actually go through with it. This child within me was a part of us.

At that same moment, I felt movement inside of me. It was as if the baby heard and understood Kim's words and tried to resist. Pretending to go along with him, I asked, "Do you have any money?"

"Well, I have a little bit from my sister," he answered.

"Give it to me. It costs money to have an abortion." Without any hesitation, he gave me what little money he had. Kim was not aware of what I was planning to use it for — to buy sleeping pills to kill myself. "Kim, give me a few days to think about it, and I suggest that you stay home for a few days to think it over, too." Kim agreed.

Living under tremendous stress and strain, I felt I had no alternative but to end my life. I was six months pregnant and I looked awful because I had not had a proper diet.

I walked into a drug store. A doctor's prescription was not necessary to obtain sedatives in Korea, so I bought some sleeping pills. There was a limit to the amount of pills I could purchase because of their potential danger. I walked to another drug store and purchased more sleeping pills, and did the same at a third drug store.

I swallowed forty-five pills. Thirty pills should have killed me. For three days, I slept soundly. When I awoke I felt angry because I had not killed myself. Confusion clouded my mind. I did not care about myself or anyone else. My unborn child was no longer a joy to me, only another burden to add to my many problems. I was so confused. Sometimes I did want the baby and other times I didn't. There were times I hoped I would have a miscarriage. Whenever the baby kicked inside me, I felt hate and contempt because the life within me was a constant reminder that all my dreams were shattered.

The growing hatred and resentment towards the child caused me to beat my stomach with my fists. I would hit myself till I could not bear the pain, but the baby continued kicking.

I screamed out in pain, "God, are you here? Can't you see what I'm going through? Where are you? Are you real?"

No matter what I did, I could not kill myself nor my baby, so I began drinking to escape the torment. In my despair, I found myself screaming and yelling. I became delirious and out of control. Then neighbors yelled back at me and told me to shut up and get out of the neighborhood because I caused such a disturbance.

Finding no relief in getting drunk, I tried one last attempt at suicide by swallowing forty-five sleeping pills with alcohol. Although I was bleeding and experiencing cramps from beating myself, death simply would not come.

When the awareness that I could not kill myself struck me, a feeling of guilt overcame me. I began to have thoughts that the baby would not be normal, so I considered having an abortion again.

I was not aware of how many days had passed since I had last seen Kim. By the time he found me in my sickened condition, he took me to the local hospital. In the hospital I feared I was losing my mind. I yelled, "Kill me! Just kill me!" Because I was hysterical and screaming in my confused state, the doctor gave me a shot to calm me down. The next thing I knew, the doctor pulled my baby out of me, three months prematurely. Our son was stillborn!

The doctor told us that he could dispose of the baby for us if we would give him more money. Kim and I did not want to give the doctor the additional money to get rid of the baby.

Through the newspapers and radios we knew that aborted babies were often found in trash cans and discarded in other unseemly ways. We did not want that to happen to our dead son, whom we wanted to have a proper burial.

Kim and I returned home in a taxi carrying our dead baby, who was wrapped in newspaper. I was extremely weak. After borrowing a neighbor's shovel, Kim searched for a decent place to bury our baby. The new shovel broke. Kim was so scared, he drank a whole bottle of whiskey to numb his mind, which was running rampant with wild thoughts.

Later that night, there was a bad storm with strong rain. I was in bed, and I trembled in fear over what I had done to my body and I also worried about the baby, knowing he was alone and helpless in the storm. When I closed my eyes, I began to see all kinds of scary sights like monsters and beast-like creatures coming to snatch me away.

Kim and I were shaking, and the storm seemed to magnify our fears. As the rain fell in torrents, I wondered if the baby would be washed away in the flooding water. I could not bear such thoughts, so I begged Kim to check the burial place. He reassured me that he had buried the body in a deep spot.

For two weeks, I could not eat. I was physically sick and mentally weak. I was confused and worn out. I began seeing things, too. When I looked at the wall, for instance, I would see my mother making Korean pancakes at the restaurant or my brother lying in bed or my sister washing clothes. Whenever I wanted to see someone, that particular person appeared before my eyes. These experiences were incredibly bizarre. I began to think I was going crazy, because I was losing touch with reality.

When I tried to sleep at night, I could see and feel the beastly creatures attacking me. They would embrace me and I could not breathe. Whether my eyes were open or closed, I was continually tormented by these apparitions.

I began to wonder if I had become some kind of medium or fortune teller. When Kim was gone, I wondered what he was doing, and exactly what he was doing would appear before my eyes. After he would return home, he would tell me what he did during the day, and it would be the same thing I saw.

I began to have frightening nightmares. Once, in a dream, my brother was beating me with a rubber water hose. He would not stop. I began screaming for him to stop, but he continued. Kim awakened me and told me I was only dreaming.

Kim returned home with money to purchase some nourishing food to help me grow stronger. Gradually, I gained a little strength to do some domestic chores. Once, as I squatted down to wash clothes in a pan, a neighbor's child noticed a pool of blood under me. He ran to his mother and told her. I was not aware that I was hemorrhaging until my neighbor informed me.

She got some towels for me, but I was bleeding uncontrollably. I even put blankets under me to soak up the blood. The loss of so much blood caused me to become light-headed and weak. Thinking that food would give me a little boost of strength, I went out to buy some bread. I fainted in the street.

My neighbor rushed me to the hospital. Since I had lost a great amount of blood, my muscles were numb and I began to have cramps. My limbs looked twisted and deformed because of the cramped muscles which lacked the proper blood circulation. The doctor gave me a shot to relax my muscles. After surgery, I was placed in a room to rest and recuperate. I was given intravenous feedings and another shot to calm me. A nurse stayed in the room with me.

I thought I would surely die in that hospital bed. I felt I was being punished for all the horrible things I had done. I then remembered the words of the preacher at the missionary school: "If you believe in Jesus, you will go to heaven. If you don't, you will go to hell." It had been a long time since I last heard those words, but now they rang clearly in my mind.

Once again, I asked, "God, are you real? If you are, then please don't let me die like this. Give me another chance. Please forgive me for the way I have lived. Make me into a new person."

Even though I asked God to help me, I kept thinking it was impossible for Him to accept me and forgive me because of my sordid life-style. Self-condemnation spoke to me: "You are a filthy sinner. There is no way God can love you. He is a holy God. He can't love you. You are too wicked to forgive."

All of a sudden the door opened and Kim walked in. Even though it was past curfew, he had been able to sneak through the dark alleys to the hospital. He asked, "Are you alright? A neighbor told me what happened." With his head leaning against the wall and seeing me in such a pitiful condition, Kim sobbed uncontrollably.

He sat on the bed beside me and stroked my pale cheek and said, "Please don't die. I want you to live. Here is some food. Please eat, kid, and gain your strength back."

I was so terribly weak, I could not respond. All I could do was cry. I just wanted to be left alone. For a good while, there was silence. Kim laid down beside me and we both drifted off to sleep.

The next day I had to go home because we lacked the money for me to stay in the hospital. I could not think for myself. I was a total mess, not even capable of making the smallest of decisions on my own. If Kim told me to sleep, I slept. If he told me to eat, I ate. I was like a zombie as I experienced a nervous breakdown. During these difficult weeks, Kim took good care of me. He cooked for me and cared for me in every way he possibly could.

As the months passed, my health slowly returned. Kim and I loved each other deeply, but we could not marry. I had to do something with my life. I knew a decision had to be made. Kim suggested that I live with one of my sisters. It seemed to be a good idea, so I decided to go to Ann's home.

When the day arrived for Kim and me to go our separate ways, it was difficult to say good-bye. Before parting, we held each other and cried. Kim said, "I love you so much. I know I have hurt and damaged you in a lot of ways, but I do love you. As much as I hate it, I must submit to my parents. I want you as my wife, but we both know that we can't marry." Then he held me tightly against him and broke down. Our hearts were breaking. Finally, he got hold of himself.

Kim drove a nail through my heart when he said, "My parents have chosen a woman for me to marry. She has an education and her family is wealthy. She is also a virgin. My parents have really encouraged me to marry her. They have promised us a new house and a new business for me." I could not stand to hear any more.

In the midst of his words of rejection, all I could do was cry. It seemed that crying was all I ever did because my heart was always hurting. Someone better than me would become Kim's wife. Even though I was the one he loved, we had to part. Was I not good enough for anyone? Was I doomed to ever be the "bad-luck crybaby?"

As I stood there with tears running down my face, I could see Kim walking further and further away from me with his head down. I yelled out to him, "You just watch!

I'm going to make it! I'm going to be somebody and you will regret that you never married me! We could make it together, Kim. You love *me*, not that other woman!" It surprised me that I was able to draw on such inner reserves of strength at such a time.

7

New Hope — A New Life

With the little money Kim gave me, I was able to travel to the small town of Munmockdong, where Ann and her family lived. As soon as I walked into her house, Ann wept for joy. She was thrilled to see me. After I shared with her all that I had been through over the past few months, she comforted me.

"It is best that you did not marry Kim. The marriage wouldn't have worked out anyway. Sounds like you are two different people," Ann counseled.

I inquired about mother and Hung Mo, and she said, "They searched and searched for you and finally gave up. Those two wearied themselves looking for you. They gave you up for dead. By the way, would you like for me to go with you to see mother and Hung Mo? I will stay right beside you when you make your peace with them."

"Oh, Ann, I am not ready for that, yet. Please, do not tell them I'm here."

Ann allowed me to stay in her home as long as I desired. She could see that I was not the same person I used to be. I was very emotional and sometimes hysterical.

I wanted to start a new life. With the money Kim gave me, I bought some new clothes and dressed up. I had hoped that this would make me feel good about myself, but I still felt very bad about myself. My self-concept was weak and I hated the person I had become.

In the evenings I would walk and walk until I spotted a bar, which I entered. I missed Kim so much. A part of me was gone. So I drank till I was drunk. This happened frequently while I lived with Ann and her family. I felt so ashamed, but I needed something to numb the gnawing pains within my heart and mind.

One day as I walked along, I came across a friend of mine from Yongsan. Hong shared with me how wonderful her life was since she had married an American. She was able to spend a great deal of money — whatever she wanted, she got. She boasted that her husband esteemed her and loved her more than life itself.

For a Korean woman to date or marry an American man was considered a shameful dishonor. The Koreans had no respect for those who did it. One day I dropped by Hong's home for help and advice. I told her about my past with the club and with Kim.

Hong said, "Do you know what you need? An American man. You need to get away from this country. You need someone to take you far away from here." Knowing how Koreans felt towards those people who go with Americans, I never thought I would allow myself to get involved with one, but Hong's words sounded appealing to me — especially the money and luxuries.

"Listen, Sun, I will talk with Mike tonight about fixing you up with one of his friends."

"Sounds good to me," I eagerly responded. One evening, the three of us were to meet one of Mike's friends. But my "blind date" never showed up. How disappointed I was.

Hong told me later that my American date was not interested in meeting me because I could not speak English. We would not have been able to communicate. For three nights, Mike and Hong took me to an American club where people met together and drank. With a five-year-old son at home, they could not continue to go out night after night.

"This is the story of my life," I thought in my self-pity. "Nobody wants me." I decided to go to the American club by myself to dance, drink and meet men. I was hoping that there would be some man at the club who would love me. To my surprise, a woman came up to me and said, "There is someone who wants to talk to you."

"What does he want?" I asked.

"He wants to know if you will dance with him."

"Sure, I will." Then the American man, whose name was Jerry, walked up to me and asked, "Do you speak English?"

I shook my head.

He said, "That's alright. No sweat, no sweat." I was capable of understanding a few basic words which I learned in high school, so I knew what he meant and smiled back at him.

After we danced for a while, he looked at me and said, "I love you and I want to marry you." I was able to understand those words and I wondered if he was crazy. He knew nothing about me or my life. We had met only a few minutes before. I wondered if this was some kind of American custom. Jerry hugged me tightly. I let him hold me and shared his affection, because I needed love.

After we sat down at a table, Jerry told an interpreter that he wanted to see me again. We continued to spend time together. One day Jerry said, "I'm stationed in Kyangjue. Will you come with me?"

In my heart, I did not love him, but I needed to belong to someone and be loved and cared for. I needed a refuge. I basked in his affection and acceptance of me. Since I could not stay with Ann forever, nor return to Mother's home, I decided to go with Jerry.

Like me, many Korean women were living with American men in Kyangjue. After a few days, three Korean women came to me. One said, "I hear that you are sleeping with a G.I. and you aren't taking any money."

"What? Why would I take his money?" I asked.

"Why would you sleep with an American without taking his money? You take all the money you can get. Strip'em clean!" she advised.

I listened intently to what she was saying. "Your G.I. has been going around saying that you do not ask for anything in return. Why are you giving to him freely?"

She informed me of the organization with which she was involved. This group, made up of Korean women, kept track of who was sleeping with whom. This group had a leader who protected the vulnerable women who were taken advantage of by the Americans. An American officer was informed of any offenses against the women.

"Listen here," she said angrily, "if you continue sleeping with that G.I. freely, you will be kicked out of this territory!"

She let me know that all the American men tried to take advantage of the women by not paying them for their services. When the men would learn of someone's free services, the other Korean women might lose their sources of income.

I let that woman know that I did not care about the money. In a rage, she pulled my hair and punched me. Looking at her, I said, "This is my life and I will do what I want to do. What I need is what I'm getting. You leave me alone!"

In my past, men had beaten and abused me, but there was no way that I was going to allow a woman to do likewise. I grabbed that woman and wrestled with her. With superhuman strength, it seemed, I beat her.

Looking at those women I declared, "Now you leave me alone. You are not going to run my life and tell me what to do. If I want to take money from an American G.I., I will take it. If I want to give all, then I will. I don't care!" Frightened, they backed off and left me alone.

The American station always provided entertainment and social events for the G.I.'s because they were lonely and away from home. Psychologically, the parties and social activities were therapeutic for the men. Jerry and I attended these gatherings frequently. One night, I drank too much and became drunk.

When we returned home, I said, "Don't touch me! I hate you and find you disgusting!" The built-up hate within me was coming out. I became violent and was swinging my arms at him. It was not Jerry I hated; it was myself. That night he slept in the barracks.

All the next day, I regretted what I had said to Jerry, and I was very sick with a hangover. I felt so guilty and depressed. Each time I drank I became violent and I would cry all the time because I was having a great self-pity party. Loneliness overtook me, for I thought Jerry would leave me.

To my relief, he returned to me that evening. When I saw my hand print on his face from slapping him the night before, all I could say was, "I'm sorry, I'm sorry!"

He was very forgiving and kind. I was so grateful that he never tried to retaliate and hurt me back. After living with Jerry for a year, he informed me that he had to return to the States. He wanted me to marry him and live in the U.S.

I thought, "I will make sure he loves me before I say yes."

"Jerry, I can't marry you."

"Why not?"

"I don't know why. I guess I don't feel worthy of you," I answered.

"Sun, if you don't marry me, then I'll kill myself." When he grabbed a rope and put it around his neck, I realized he was serious.

Many times I had tested his love for me. He certainly had strange ways of showing that he loved me.

I thought, "Who am I to turn down someone who would take me to the United States and take care of me?

Why would I turn down a man who would take his life for me? This opportunity would provide me with a brand-new start in a new land."

Finally, I responded, "Honey, if you love me that much, I can't say no to you. As soon as you go back to the States, send the government a visa request and I will be right there." Jerry was so happy that he jumped up and down. He picked me up in his arms and swung me around.

To make our engagement official, Jerry wanted to meet my family and tell them the good news. I was very hesitant to go back home. Meeting my family was very important to Jerry because he felt that the commitment between the two of us would be stronger if he could meet my family.

I requested that Ann go before me, as a peacemaker, to mother and Hung Mo. Ann informed the family of my future plans with Jerry: "Jerry and Sun would like to announce their engagement to you. You can meet and also say good-bye to Sun."

Hung Mo refused to see me. He wanted to forget that he knew me. Ann sadly told me the news, "Sun, I'm so sorry, but you cannot return home. You are not welcome there any more." Jerry continued to press the issue, refusing to take no for an answer.

I decided to take it upon myself to arrange a meeting between my fiance and my family. I walked close to the marketplace where mother worked. I saw a young boy, and gave him some money to tell my mother where I was. She came out to see me. It was the first time we had seen each other in two and a half years. She was shocked to see me. With tears flowing down my face, I said, "Mother, I beg you, please forgive me. Please!" I begged mother to accept me, and I explained my future plans to her.

Mother cried along with me and said, "You'd better leave fast! If your brother sees you, he will kill you. Run!"

"Mother! Mother!" I cried. "What can I do to make peace before I leave to go overseas? I don't want to leave like this."

"Honey," she answered, "I will talk to Hung Mo on your behalf, but I can't promise you anything."

A week later, Jerry and I went to the PX to buy a couple of sacks of American food for mother and Hung Mo. The food represented a peace offering. As Jerry and I approached my mother's house, I realized I was taking a risk by confronting Hung Mo, but I thought Jerry would protect me.

When I came face to face with Hung Mo, he simply did not look at me. He did not speak a word. My mother did not know what to do, she kept silent and waited to see what my brother was going to do. The contention between Hung Mo and me did not seem to bother Jerry. Boldly, Jerry pulled out a gold ring, placed it on my finger, and smiled from ear to ear. He was so happy.

About a week later, Jerry left Korea and returned to the United States. We were apart for five months, waiting on the immigration paperwork to be completed.

8

Life in the Promised Land

In April of 1972, I arrived in the United States, leaving
my past behind. I wanted to begin a new life. The plane
landed in Indianapolis, Indiana, where Jerry and his
parents met me. He introduced me to his parents, and I
was grateful to claim them as my parents, too. It was
wonderful to have a father, since I had never known one.
We got acquainted over drinks. I tried so hard for mom
and dad to like me.

As Jerry and I walked together, hand in hand, his
parents followed us. I had the strangest intuition that they
did not accept me. I tried to figure out the reason for their
displeasure towards me; maybe I was ugly, or they
disliked the affection that Jerry and I showered on each
other. I became paranoid and felt strongly that they were
talking about me, negatively. I could not escape those
feelings.

As we entered the car, I heard them mention the words, "mini-skirt." Mom and Dad disapproved of my short skirt! They did not seem to be the type of Americans I expected them to be. I expected Americans to be "foot-loose and fancy free." I thought anything was acceptable to Americans, but my expectations were wrong.

In the car, fear rose in my heart because I knew I gave them a poor first impression. My heart pounded from nervousness and anxiety. Jerry's parents thought I spoke only Korean. They continued to talk about me as if I could not understand any English. They said, "What kind of girl is she? She sure must be wild wearing such a short skirt." What I did understand let me know of their disapproval.

When we arrived in New Castle, Indiana, I was surprised that mom gave me a tour of their little home. In Korea, this was not done. I was impressed with the big beds because I had been used to sleeping on the floor. The dining room was so pretty, and I was amazed to see a twenty-five-inch color television set, which I had never seen before.

For two weeks, Jerry and I lived with his parents. I had to make some adjustments to life in this new land. For one thing, I could not eat American food, so I prepared Korean meals for myself. Mom and dad, however, were repulsed by the smell of it.

Opening the doors and windows, mom said, "This stuff stinks! How can you eat this kind of food? I do not see how you can stand it. Don't forget to brush your teeth after eating this nasty stuff. Yuck!"

Bound up as I was with years of fear and rejection, their words added more pain to my deep-rooted feelings. I felt so nervous and insecure around them. Whenever Jerry and his dad went to work on the night shift, at the automobile factory, I would stay in our bedroom, afraid to venture out. Feelings of paranoia paralyzed me. I felt no freedom in that household.

Late at night, while mom slept, I would sneak into the kitchen to prepare Korean food. I tried to be as quiet as a mouse so she would not be disturbed. One night, much to my dismay, mom came out to the kitchen and opened the windows, complaining of the smell. Her attitude hurt me and I lost my appetite.

I did not feel free to speak in front of mom and dad, either. Since my English was not fluent, I would combine Korean and English words. Since Jerry had lived in Korea for a while, he had no problem understanding me, but mom and dad were greatly disturbed by it. They told me not to jabber in Korean and not to eat Korean food. It seemed that anything related to Korea was forbidden by them.

At times on television there would be shows with various Oriental people. If a pretty Oriental female appeared on the screen, mom would make a comment like, "She must be Japanese," or, "She must be from Thailand." In order to hurt me, she made derogatory remarks in front of me. Then, whenever an ugly Oriental female was shown, mom would sarcastically remark, "She must be Korean!"

Jerry was my rock of security during this time of adjustment. I did not want him to leave me, but he had to go to work at night and sleep during the day. So, I occupied my lonely days with television and correspondence to my family overseas.

During my first week of living in the United States, I had fantasies of my wedding day. I pictured lots of guests and gifts and goodies to eat. I dreamed of a beautiful, white wedding gown and an elaborate ceremony. It excited me to ponder our wedding in the United States — it would be marvelous!

After living in New Castle for one week, Jerry came home and told me to put a dress on because we were to get married that day. I did not understand the rush. We had not discussed it, nor made any kind of wedding plans. "But, Jerry what kind of dress?"

"It does not matter. Just any dress." I ended up wearing my mini-skirt to a huge church to get married.

The church was large. It had rows and rows of pews, but only mom and dad attended. I was very disillusioned. The minister came out to greet the four of us. He said a few words which I did not understand. Jerry said, "Yes, I do."

The minister wanted me to say the same thing, so I said, "I do."

After Jerry kissed me, we went home. There were no gifts, no reception, no guests. I wondered what kind of wedding we had had. Where was the America Jerry talked about? The loving family and the beautiful home filled with luxuries?

Next door, there was a sweet Christian woman who came over to see me after Jerry and I were married. She gave me a candy jar with a dish towel inside. That was the only wedding gift I received. Mom and dad gave me nothing, not even a hug or a kind word.

I was so touched by this precious lady who showed me kindness. She told me about Jesus and that she attended the church where I was married. She also hugged me and let me know she loved me. I felt closer to her than to mom and dad. She told me that I was a beautiful girl and that she enjoyed being with me. Because of her tender love, I broke down and cried.

I only wished that mom and dad would feel the same way towards me. I became annoyed with them for treating me like a child. They were always watching me. As each day passed, I learned more English and understood their talks about me.

After I found out that there were some Koreans living in the same city, I wanted to call and meet them. I thought it would be great to get acquainted and have some people to talk to. Mom refused to allow me to make any calls to them.

She said, "If you speak English, then you may call. If you plan to speak Korean, then forget it. I do not want you jabbering in Korean. For all I know, you may be talking about us!"

It did not take me long to learn of mom and dad's prejudices. There was a black girl who delivered their newspaper in the evenings. Because of her color, they quit buying the paper. They did not want any blacks on their property.

During the second week of my stay, mom took me to a few garage sales. I purchased some silverware, dishes and clothes.

Finally, after two weeks of living under the same roof with mom and dad, Jerry and I moved into our own little house. Jerry had to teach me how to cook and clean because the food preparation and domestic chores were so different from Korean ways. All of this was new to me.

I grew weary of going to mom and dad's each evening with Jerry, who seemed to have nothing better to do. I felt only rejection there. They were prejudiced against Koreans. Each time we returned home, Jerry and I ended up in an argument. His parents had a way of bringing out the worst in us because they tried to control us.

In June of 1972, Jerry and I were expecting our first child. Both of us were thrilled with the news. Jerry went to the stores to buy maternity clothes for me. He treated me royally and helped me with the cooking and cleaning.

Since Jerry and I had no phone, we went to mom and dad's one fall evening to use theirs. Mom was busy at the kitchen table counting a pile of pennies. When I asked for permission to use the phone, mom asked me who I was going to call. I told her that I wanted to talk to my Korean friends. Again, she refused to allow me to make any calls if I spoke Korean.

"But, mom!" I said, "My friends do not know English very well. Besides, I cannot speak good English."

She looked at me and demanded, "You live in America, and you are going to have an American baby. You are not Korean any more!"

I shot back, "I may have an American baby and I may live in America, but I cannot be an American woman! I still have Korean blood in me."

Mom became furious with me and shouted, "I do not like for anybody to talk back to me! You will not talk back to me. I will not allow it, nor tolerate it. You get out right now!" Then she wiped the table with her arm and cleared the pennies off. Her face was red with anger!

She continued, "If you don't stop eating Korean food and speaking that Korean language, then you are not welcome here!"

I was not accepted in my own country and I was not accepted in this new country. I was crushed. The feelings of rejection rose up again. With tears welling in my eyes, I said, "Oh, mom, I did not mean to hurt you by talking back to you."

She said, "No one talks back to me! My three sons have never talked back to me, and you are not going to talk back to me. Now, get out of here!"

Leaving my shoes and Jerry behind, I fled from the house. I did not even know how to get back to our home. Jerry heard the commotion and got in his car to find me. When he located me, I was so upset and angry from many pent-up emotions that I took it out on him. "Sun, come here! Get in the car!"

"No! You leave me alone," I said and stomped away in a fit of rage, gritting my teeth. I was furious with Jerry. I blamed him for the hurt and rejection I felt in America.

Jerry grabbed me, picked me up and put me in the car. All the way home, I cried and cried. The minute I walked inside, I began throwing dishes and shoes and anything within my reach at Jerry. I was out of control.

"Stop it, honey. You are hurting yourself! You are hurting the baby. Please, I beg you, stop it! Stop it!" he shouted.

Through the years, anger and rejection had snowballed and lodged inside of me until something came along to them, triggered and set me off in an explosive reaction which only magnified those emotions. The feelings of hurt and rejection were compounded by the feeling that I had been cheated and deceived.

My conception of America had always been that Americans had anything they wanted whenever they wanted it. I thought this land was full of rich people and bountiful prosperity. I was disillusioned and disappointed. I thought Jerry had everything he needed and wanted, too. But I was wrong. I became sick and tired of being poor and of having my hopes deferred and dashed on the rocks of disappointment.

Jerry was deeply in debt. Because of his two previous marriages and child support, he was financially strapped. In one marriage, he and his ex-wife had filed for bankruptcy. He had to borrow money from his parents each week to buy gas and cigarettes.

I manipulated Jerry with my emotions. I refused to sleep with him for three days. And no matter where he was, I made sure I was elsewhere. If he was in the living room, then I remained in the bedroom. If he came into the bedroom, I went to another room.

For ten days, we stayed away from his parents. Seeing that I was really mad, they came over to our house with a coat they had bought at a rummage sale for me. Even though they had paid only a dollar for the coat, their gesture warmed my heart. At last they considered my feelings and saw my need. Also, I felt that I had conquered them because they came to us first. We acted as though nothing had happened and became at least civil to one another.

On December 19 the doctor told me that our baby was due. Later that day, however, I went into labor. I told my friend next door who said, "Sounds like you are ready to have the baby."

"But the doctor said that I was not due until next month," I objected.

"Well, honey, the doctor is not always right. He can miss it too. So you'd better be careful and start timing your contractions." I agreed to be careful. I had such a strong urge to clean and work. I kept myself occupied, and then I noticed that the contractions were getting closer and closer.

A few hours later, at 7:06 am, on December 20, 1972, I gave birth to a black-headed, beautiful boy. Our little Jody was born three weeks premature.

On December 22, I went home. I was losing a great deal of blood and my body was swelling. By Christmas day, I was still passing blood. I was very pale and growing steadily weaker. I nearly passed out. Jerry took me to the emergency room. I was given a D & C and a blood transfusion.

Whenever Jerry or the nurses came into my room, I cried out to them, begging for life. Around midnight, as a last resort, I cried out to God once more: "God, I am afraid I am going to die, but I am not ready to go. I know I will not make it to heaven. Please don't let me die. If you let me live, I will do anything. I will take my baby to church and I promise to serve you. Please give me another chance."

Over and over, throughout that night, I begged God for life. With plenty of time to think, I considered what

my Mother had gone through in giving birth to me. Since
I had experienced childbirth that week, I was able to
empathize with her. I felt a tremendous, overwhelming
love for mother — deeper than I had ever experienced
before. I desired to tell her of my love and to show Jody to
her, but I felt that I would never have such an
opportunity. Because of these feelings, I felt extremely
depressed and lonely.

Four days later, I was taken back home. I grew
stronger and stronger as each day passed. My
commitment to God was short-lived. For three Sundays
Jerry and I went to church with mom and dad. Since they
were not regular attenders, Jerry and I quit going, too. I
thought that going to church was serving God. I did not
realize that serving the Lord was a day-to-day
relationship.

9

Sweet Revenge

In the summer of 1974, Jerry granted me permission to visit my family in Korea. We could not afford the flight, so we borrowed the money. Jerry stayed home and worked. My purpose in visiting home was to show my family, friends, and especially Kim that I had made something of myself. I was a wife and a mother. I was so excited to show my son off, who was one and a half years old.

My family was glad to see me. Time had served as a healer of our relationships. Even Hung Mo, who was married and a father, accepted me. He was still sick, but was capable of getting up and around a little better than before. The family reunions were wonderful, but I longed to see Kim and prove myself to him. Ann's husband arranged for Kim and me to meet at a teahouse. Kim was shocked when he found out I was in the vicinity, but he definitely wanted to see me. We had not seen each other for nearly four years.

As the two of us sat across from each other, I told him that I was married, had a son, and had been living in the United States for two and a half years. Kim did not believe me.

"Look at this, Kim," I said as I pulled out my passport.

"Well, check it out! You really have come from there," he responded with surprise.

We proceeded to talk about our lives and our families. I was relieved to hear what Kim had to share. He said, "You know, Sun, I have a confession to make to you. I lied about being sterile. I am the proud father of a beautiful little girl who is Jody's age. The baby you were carrying when we were living together was ours.

"Whenever I passed the village where we buried the baby, I would be so guilt-ridden that I would stop at a bar and buy a drink. It really bothered me to pass that place.

"And another thing, Sun, the woman I married is a good woman, but nothing like you. We have our share of problems. You were always so passive and submissive, but Omi stands up to me and we clash a lot.

"I know it's too late to say this, but I really regret what happened between the two of us. I guess you were right all along. You said I would regret it, and I do."

I gloated. It felt great to hear Kim admit that he lied to me, and that he regretted our splitting up. It did me good to hear all that.

After we had visited for a while, Kim suggested that we go to a motel and spend more time together. I flatly refused his offer. Being married, I was not going to take this risk. Kim became irate with me like a spoiled child. I was not going to allow him to control me like he had in the past. I felt that I had won a great victory as I walked away from him. I had gotten my revenge; I had hurt Kim by rejecting him as he had done to me four years earlier.

While in Korea, Jody had a difficult time adjusting to the food. He had diarrhea so bad that I decided to take him to the hospital. As we left, I noticed Kim standing at the corner close to mother's home. When he spotted us, he came up to me to talk. I said, "I'm glad for you, Kim. You married the woman you wanted. You now have a daughter, and your family is established. There is nothing left between us. You told me a week ago all that I needed to hear — by admitting to me that the baby was yours. We have nothing left to say. We are finished."

As we left the hospital, Kim followed us. I told him to leave me alone. Seeing that I was serious, he consented and never bothered me again.

Soon after that incident, my sister Ann saw Omi, Kim's wife. Her face was covered with marks and bruises from Kim's abuse. Kim had vented his anger and frustration on her. Obviously, I had gotten to him. I was so satisfied with my revenge, even though it had cost his wife physical pain.

Jody's first birthday, December 1973
Dressed in traditional Korean outfit.

Jody age 5 — Tejay age 2

Top Row (L to R): Sister Ann, Mama Lee, Sister Cha, Brother Hung Mo.
Bottom Row (L to R): Sister Ock, Sun, Phun

Sun in traditional Korean dress, taken just
before coming to the states.

10

The Turning Point

I returned to New Castle, Indiana. Jerry and I were still
in debt. To pay off the loan for my trip to Korea, I started
working at a sewing factory. After the seven-year penalty
from his bankruptcy had passed, Jerry was able to
establish credit again,so we went on shopping sprees and
bought items beyond our budget. I loved having new
furniture and clothes. Even though we charged a great
deal, and were in debt, I felt we were rich just because we
had nice things in the home.

For the next few months, our little household was
happy and content. To add to our joy, I became pregnant
again. I was so pleased to be carrying another child, but I
was deeply concerned about my health. My last two
pregnancies had been so difficult. I thought it would be
helpful if my mother could come to the States to live with
us and assist me with the house and children. In this way,

my dream would be fulfilled by being able to support my
mother who had to sacrifice so much in her life. Jerry
agreed to this plan.

The immigration office granted my request and
allowed my mother to come and live with us. In the
spring of 1975, when I was six months pregnant, mother
arrived. I noticed that Jerry was not as loving and
affectionate as he used to be. I figured it was because I
was so big with our child. He would not even tell me he
loved me like he used to. My friends told me that they
had seen him with another woman, but I refused to
believe it. I knew better, because Jerry would die for me. I
knew his love for me was strong.

There were times when the phone rang and the caller
would hang up when mother answered. Mother
remarked, "It is so strange — the phone rings a dozen
times a day and the caller never speaks. It is very
disturbing." Mother sensed very strongly that something
was wrong.

"Oh, mother," I said, as reassuringly as I could,
"people cannot understand you, so they hang up. It is just
you."

"No, Sun. I have a bad feeling that there is something
definitely wrong. Also, I have noticed that whenever I am
in the same room as Jerry, when he is on the phone, he
avoids me and leaves the room. It is as if he is guilty
about something or he's trying to hide something from
me.

"Now, mother, do not talk like that. I trust Jerry and I
know he loves me."

On August 10, 1975, at 9:00 am, I gave birth to TeJay,
a healthy ten-pound boy. Even though the doctor was

prepared, I lost a lot of blood again. Because I had not kept my word to God, I was afraid to ask for His help this time. I had broken my promise to live for God and I had not remained true to my commitment. I had continued to live my life my own way.

After TeJay's birth, Jerry's attitude continued to be cold towards me. I was continually hearing people say that they saw him drinking in bars with other women. When I confronted him, he always denied it. I could not prove it, but I could feel his coldness towards me.

Life should have been grand for me. Jerry and I were both working. We had two healthy, beautiful boys with a house full of nice furniture. Mother was helping with the cooking and babysitting, but still there was something missing in my life. There was a void inside me and I was unhappy. I found myself still battling the fear of death. On the outside, my family and I looked happy and loving; but on the inside, neither Jerry nor I were truly content with ourselves, or each other. I found myself bickering at Jerry and the boys over everything.

Spending time with friends provided a good outlet for me. One Korean girl friend, Loti, who worked at the sewing factory, was having terrible marital problems. She was battling deep depression. Her husband, Larry, was attending church whenever the doors opened, but Loti had no desire to join him. This caused a lot of conflict between them.

I encouraged her to attend the church meetings with her husband, thinking it would do her some good. "No thanks," Loti responded. "I used to go, but there is nothing for me at church. It does not do a thing for me. I do not want any part of it."

Not long afterwards, I learned that Loti was in the hospital. I went to see her. She had lost her appetite and was down to eighty-five pounds. She was very thin and she had an I.V. in her arm for feeding. She was lonely and could not receive love from her husband and her son. Like me, she was insecure, fearful and miserable. We were like two peas in a pod, and I wanted to help her.

"Loti, I hear that the church is having a revival this week. If I go, will you go with me?" I was not concerned about myself and my marriage, but my concern was for Loti and her marriage. I buried myself in her problems, ignoring mine.

"My goodness, Sun. I am a Christian. I am supposed to invite you to church. You are not even a Christian and you are asking me."

"Well," I said."You ought to go. Look at yourself. You look awful. I do not like to see you so unhappy. Why don't you go with your husband to church?"

"He is too involved, I cannot stand it," she replied.

When Loti grew stronger and was discharged from the hospital, she agreed to join me for church one night. J.D. Redman was the guest speaker. I will never forget his message; it was as though he was speaking directly to me.

He said, "When everything is going smooth we forget God. But, when we become desperate enough, we cry out to Him and make all kinds of promises to Him."

"My, oh, my," I reflected. "That is the way I have been." I began to recall the times I made vain promises to serve God in my times of desperation.

He gave a poignant illustration just before he gave the altar call: "There was a little girl who was in an accident.

Her parents cried out for God to heal their daughter. They said they would be faithful to God if he did so. God healed their daughter, but it did not take long before the parents' love for God waxed cold. The little girl became ill. The parents cried out, saying that they would do anything for God if only He would heal her. Again, God healed the little girl. When the parents became comfortable again in the good times they forgot the Lord.

"The child was afflicted a third time. This time, she was hit by a car and was killed. As the child lay in the casket, her parents blamed God for taking their daughter. They wondered why God would do such a terrible thing. What the parents did not realize was that God had granted their first two requests. It seems that whenever people make a vow to God, then break it and face their consequences, they tend to blame God for all their troubles. God was faithful and answered their prayers, but they willfully turned away from Him."

J.D. looked at us with compassion in his eyes and said, "If that were your child in the casket, it would be too late to pray. Do not wait until it is too late to pray. Do not wait until you are desperate to pray. If you have made a commitment in the past, keep it. If you promised God you would serve Him, then serve Him...."

I began to think about my promises to serve God after I gave birth to Jody. I remembered reaching out to the people who entered my room and I cried out to them for life. Then, when all was quiet, I cried out to God and promised Him I would serve Him. J.D.'s words quickened my heart.

I also thought about the times when I tried to take my life, but God had spared me and had allowed me to come to America. After my abortion in Korea I thought I could not have children, but God blessed me with two sons and a husband who loved me.

I started to cry. I wanted to go up front and surrender my life to the Lord, but I could not get out of my seat. I felt an overwhelming oppression against me. A woman I knew from the sewing factory looked at me and said, "May I go up front with you?"

I don't know how I did it, but I managed to go forward with this woman. Loti came up to the altar, too, and she rededicated her life to the Lord. We both asked the Lord to forgive us and to cleanse us of our pasts. I asked Jesus to make His abode in my heart. What peace and joy I had. I felt so clean and pure and free!

I went home with a smile on my face and told Jerry that I was born again. He did not have much to say. It was no big deal to him. Whenever I asked him to come to church with me, he refused and said he was not ready. Sadly enough, we seemed to fight and argue after I came home from church.

Three weeks after I was saved, I had a dream. Two policemen where chasing me. The policemen had a gun and they were planning to kill me. As I tried to escape, I came against a wall of fire. I noticed a passageway which I entered. It led to a pit which was huge and pitch-dark and it was filled with snakes and worms. I noticed that I was covered with black grime and filth. I also experienced tremendous thirst. Greater was my desire to find something to drink than to escape the slimy pit. Although I could not stand going into the pit, I heard myself cry out, "I am so thirsty! I want some water —*water!*"

All of a sudden I was out of the pit and I beheld a mountain. About half way up the mountain a fountain of water was flowing. It appeared so clear and clean and appealing. As I began to climb the mountain to get to the fountain, I had difficulty because the ground was slippery. I fell time and time again, but kept trying to climb. Finally, I reached the fountain. I immersed myself in the water, and drank and drank. To my horror, a black force came before me and prevented me from quenching my thirst. At this point I woke up.

I remembered being told as a child that when police chased a person in a dream, it was symbolic of Satan's messengers chasing a person into hell. The pit had represented hell. The mountain had signified Jesus and the fountain represented the Holy Spirit. I was partaking of the living water. But an evil force had stopped me from drinking.

That dream spoke loudly and clearly to me. The black force that prevented me from drinking was my husband. He would always find some issue to argue about every time I came home from church feeling refreshed and happy. He quenched my joy and I gave in to the bickering, too. The tension between us continued to grow.

Three months after I became a Christian, Jerry asked for a divorce. We had been married for only four years. His request came as a shock to me. I could not believe he wanted a divorce. "Don't you want me, Jerry? I thought you loved me!" I shouted at him.

He said, "I'm tired of fussing and fighting. I don't want to live this way any more."

To get back at him, I called his parents to let them know what was going on. I wanted them to know that Jerry was "the jerk" in this case and I was the innocent one. I wanted them on my side. Mom and dad came right over after I talked to them. I also called Jerry's brother and sister-in-law, and they drove out to see us too. There was a lot of yelling among all of us in the small house.

Dad said, "Jerry, enough is enough! You are supporting one ex-wife and two kids. Do you want to support another wife and two more kids? Don't be foolish! Try to work out your differences this time."

"What kind of man are you? Can't you be satisfied with one woman?" his brother, Dennis, shouted. "You have had three wives!"

With the family all involved, I told Jerry to get out and never come back.

"I will, don't worry." Jerry shouted in frustration. Then he threatened, "Tomorrow I plan to go the prosecutor's office!"

Before he could leave, with all the confusion and fussing and fighting, our parents' health was affected. His dad's bad heart could not tolerate much more stress and strain. An ambulance came and the medics gave oxygen. He was experiencing chest pains. My mother was in another room hyperventilating.

Later in the evening, Jerry's family left. When the "dust" had settled and all was quiet, with mother resting in bed, Jerry and I were able to work things out and he decided to stay. Because we talked most of the night, he did not go to work for his shift.

The following day, after I came home from work, my mother said, "Sometimes we expect too much from men and we expect them to make the first move. There are times the man likes for the woman to be aggressive. Sun, I advise you to shower affection on Jerry. Don't wait for him to come to you first. Tell him you love him and give him a lot a love."

Mother was brought up to serve her husband and to put him first. She told me to serve Jerry and that it was not too late to make the marriage work.

Deep inside I carried resentment towards Jerry, but I decided to accept mother's wise counsel. I hid my feelings, walked into the bedroom, and suggested to Jerry that we go to bed together. He was shocked, because we had had such a bad fight the night before and I had never been aggressive with my affection in this way.

Jerry was very pleased by my request. We got into bed and talked and loved each other. Before long the phone rang. I answered it, but the other person hung up, this happened twice. The phone rang again, but this time I gave the receiver to Jerry. The room was so quiet that I was able to hear a woman's voice say, "What has been going on?"

Jerry whispered, "After a while." I quickly grabbed the phone and said, "Hello!" but the woman hung up on me. My heart started pounding like a drum. I knew that this was more serious than I ever realized.

I looked directly at Jerry. Trying to control myself, I said, "If you tell the whole truth, we can start over, but if you don't, then we will be finished, tonight!"

Jerry confessed to me that he had met this woman when I was in Korea for a couple of months. She had been his high-school sweetheart. When she got divorced, Jerry had gotten together with her. They were both lonely. For over a year, they had been having an affair. He had been supporting her. He had time to spend with her while I was working during the day. She confronted Jerry to make a decision — to choose her or me. It was then that I realized why he had asked me for a divorce. I threw the same question back to him: "Jerry, what are you going to do? Who do you want?"

He chose to stay with me. Inside, I was like a raging volcano; I wanted him to stay with me until I could get even. I was not going to let him go that easily. I felt like killing him — how dare he reject me! I forgot God again and all I wanted was revenge!

Later that night, after Jerry left for work, I once again considered suicide; this would be my revenge to Jerry. By killing myself, I figured he would feel responsible for my death and live in constant torment. I hated him.

Early the next morning, I went to a park. Being of a stubborn nature, I decided to deprive my body of food and water. Pills did not kill me before, so now I would try this method. I told God that I hated Him and everybody else. I erroneously assumed that everything would be peachy after I turned my life over to Him, but actually things turned out to be much worse.

Blaming God for all my woes, I said, "God, I cannot handle the mess my life is in. I gave you my life, but this is too much for me. I am going to kill myself. Please just let me die. Don't stop me!"

I cried and agonized all morning. After wearing myself out, I could not cry any more. As I sat quietly for a while, I heard the Lord speak to my heart, *"Examine yourself."* God wanted me to understand the reasons for my behavior and attitudes towards people and circumstances. I began to see why I was so unhappy. I had brought trouble and grief upon myself — I had driven Jerry away from me.

The Lord reminded me of how much Jerry used to love me. I had always felt better and smarter than him, so I had criticized and belittled him. From the things he said, and his decisions, I did not think Jerry had it "all together," so I began to lose respect for him.

As I continued to search my heart, I saw how wrong I was by neglecting to love Jerry. I was full of pride, selfishness, manipulation, anger, hurt, bitterness, and rejection. I could not stand the thought of more rejection after I had really opened my heart and shared my life with Kim. It was a losing battle for Jerry to love me.

While in Vietnam, Jerry had been rejected by a woman whom he dearly loved and admired. That is the reason he was determined to make our engagement official in front of my family before he returned to the States. Like me, he suffered the emotional pain of rejection. I deceived myself into thinking that I would be able to escape my past and enter into a brand-new life, but that was impossible because I could not escape *myself*; the battle and feelings within tormented me no matter where I lived. After I saw the garbage inside of me, I asked the Lord what I should do. As I stood in the park, the Lord showed me that I was the one who needed to change.

The Lord told me to forgive all the people who had hurt me in my past. This included my family, friends and Jerry. I cried and asked the Lord how to forgive Jerry, the pain he caused me. God spoke to me and said, I have forgiven you, now you have to forgive him. I began to see how filthy I was on the inside. I even thought God would zap me — I was scared of Him. All I could do was cry and agonize with my face on the ground. I repented of all the hate and bitterness within me. I was sorrowful about the selfishness in my life and for not caring about my family and loved ones.

As I broke before the Lord, I realized I had been unfaithful to God time and time again. Even though I had been born again, my life did not glorify God. The Lord had always waited for me to turn to Him and spend time with Him, but I trudged through life my own way. I had hurt myself, mistreated others, and grieved God.

While still in my mother's womb, I had been branded with rejection. People felt I would only be an added burden after the death of my father. I was a "bad-luck baby."

That day, God set me free from those feelings of rejection and cleansed me. He set me free from my sin. I felt like a new person. The thirst in my dreams had been quenched. I hurried home to tell Jerry how God had changed me and how sorry I was for how I had treated him. Around 4:00 pm, I knelt beside Jerry's bed. He was sleeping soundly. "Jerry, Jerry wake up," I said gently. "Will you forgive me?" He opened his eyes in shock. Never had I ever humbled myself before him.

He was the one who always apologized first during our four years of marriage, whenever we argued. Even when I was at fault, I took advantage and manipulated him by rejecting him until he came to me.

With tears streaming down my face, I cried, "Honey, I beg you to forgive me. I'm sorry for treating you so badly and causing so much grief in our marriage. I do love you. I've been wrong and selfish. I'm sorry for not making you feel special. Please give me another chance to be a good wife to you. With God's help we can make it."

He sat up in bed, still shocked. He had never seen me like that before. Feeling guilty because of his affair, Jerry said, "Stop it, honey. It's not you. I promise you that I won't see that woman any more and I will attend church with you."

The following Sunday was Easter. He gave his life to the Lord on that day. For the next three months, we felt like we were on a honeymoon. We were doing great!

Larry and Sun Fannin. Engagement in 1980.

Sun at Prayer Mtn. in Spencer Ind. in 1987.

Sister Ann and Mama Lee in 1980 at our wedding.

11

God Supplies All My Needs

After the three months passed, Jerry began making excuses before church services on Sundays and Wednesdays. "I have a headache." "I have to go to work early." "I don't feel good." "I'll go next week." Before long, Jerry was back in the arms of another woman. Then there were other girl friends in his life —not just one, but two, then three, and then four...

People informed me that he was seen in bars with various women. He drove around using his C.B. to talk to and entice women. He went wild.

Because of my strong desire to live for God and my renewed love for Jerry, I did not allow his roaming around to affect me as it used to. I was amazed at the change inside me — outward circumstances did not pull me down. I was walking in joy and victory! People thought I was crazy for wanting him, but I loved him so much.

God had also delivered me from the fear of death. One bad, snowy day in the winter of 1977, I knew beyond any doubt I was free of this tormenting fear. A friend and I were driving home from work; we had to drive about ten or twenty miles per hour because the ice was thick. All of a sudden, as we were heading eastward, a vehicle in front of us slid into the ditch. My friend, Betty, became scared and automatically applied her foot to the brake. Our car spun around and we were facing in the opposite direction. Betty was shaking so hard; a big truck headed towards us and barely missed our car as it passed by. We thought we were going to have a head-on collision with that truck. As I sat beside her, I gently laid my hand on her arm and prayed. I had such peace inside! "Jesus, I thank you for protecting us."

As Betty sat trembling, I got out and directed her to turn the car around. She then parked the car in the emergency lane. Then I walked to the car in the ditch. With snow up to my waist, I asked the woman in the ditch if she was alright. She answered, "Yes."

I offered to shovel her out, but my efforts to shovel were in vain. The snow was so deep and the air so extremely cold that it was impossible to accomplish anything at all. Snow kept falling in the spots I cleared.

The thought that I should pray occurred to me. I put the shovel down and put my hand on the car. I prayed in faith, "God, nothing is impossible with you. You can do all things mightily. I know you can get this car out of the ditch. With man it's impossible, but with you all things are possible."

I told the lady to try to drive out of the ditch.

"I have tried, but I can't get out!" I continued my direction, "I believe you will now. Try it again!" The instant the woman turned the key, the car started and she drove out of the ditch. I had never experienced such a miraculous answer to prayer! We were thrilled. She kept thanking me over and over. I said, "Don't thank me. Jesus did it. Thank Jesus. I just prayed."

After I returned to Betty's car, she was still "shaken up," but I thought I would burst with joy! I was so excited to see what God could do!

We resumed our trip home. I began singing and praising the Lord with tears flowing down my face. "What are you doing?" she asked.

"Joy is welling up and it's hard to contain myself because I know that God has delivered me from the fear of death," I replied with confidence.

Normally Betty would mock me whenever I gave God praise, but this time, she watched me for a while with a sober expression on her face. She said, "You know, Sun, I see a big difference in your life. I see that it's not you, but God is real in your life. You've got something inside that is genuine."

I responded to her comments by showing gratitude to her: "I also know that I've been spared death because of your prayers for me. I've had some close calls with death, but God has protected me each time. I probably would've been killed if you weren't with me today." The next Sunday, Betty and her mother went to church and dedicated their lives to the Lord.

During the summer of 1978, Jerry asked me for a separation. He suggested that I find a lawyer. I did not understand any legal procedures, but Jerry wanted to be fair in dividing our belongings. "I don't want a divorce, Jerry."

"We aren't getting a divorce. We're only separating, but I need a few things to live. So, you find out from your lawyer the amount of money I need to send for support and how often I can be with the boys."

As I discussed all this with my lawyer, he suggested that Jerry come for an appointment to sign the papers. Sadly, I signed the papers too, although I did not fully understand the American legal terms.

With Jerry renting an apartment, the cash flow dwindled dramatically in my household. Jerry neglected to send me the promised support money, and I was unable to make payments on our house which we had purchased the previous year. With the telephone disconnected, the food supply getting low, all my household bills fell behind and again the debts grew.

I remained faithful in tithing my income each week. I prayed about our financial situation, yet the pressure remained. People sensed that the boys and I were going through a crucial time. Mother did not want to add to my pressures, so she didn't tell me when we ran out of rice. She prepared noodles for dinner for three days. The boys complained to me about eating the same thing.

"Mother, prepare some rice for the boys sometime, please."

Bursting into tears, mother said, "We don't have meat or rice or any vegetables, Sun. I didn't want to burden you with more problems."

"Mother, the boys have to eat properly. All I know to do is to pray." I went to a bedroom and cried out to God and stood on Phillipians 4:19 which says, "God shall supply all my needs according to His riches in glory in Christ Jesus." The next day a lady brought us two sacks of groceries! One sack was full of beef and the other had canned foods. Sometimes people from a Korean church which I had attended drove over fifty miles to bring us rice. Over and over, people brought us food or gave us money. Our needs were always met.

One Sunday, I had $20.00 to my name. With many pressing needs at home, I was tempted not to give it as unto the Lord. I battled within myself and began to bargain with God. "Lord, I need this money. Do I have to give it? I don't want to."

In my heart, I knew the tithes belonged to Him and that He would take care of me. So I obeyed and gave it. After arriving home from church, Jody told me that he was going to get the mail. "Jody, this is Sunday. We don't get mail today." He insisted on getting the mail and took off running to the mailbox. When he returned to the house, he handed me an envelope which contained a check in the amount of $80.00! God was always watching over us. He rewards obedience. During times like this, I was learning to trust Him.

For nearly sixty years, mother had served Buddha. She had been a strong believer and had spent much money paying the priest to pray to Buddha for Hung Mo's healing. Mother continued to pray to Buddha when she came to the States, although there was no temple where she could worship. Mother had been in the States for two years and was very lonely. Although she understood no English, she began going to church with me.

After a year of attending services with me, one morning at church, she cried and cried until I became embarrassed. "Mother, why are you crying so much?" I whispered.

"Can't you see somebody out there by the piano?"

"Who?"

She went on, "There's a man standing there and, with His hand outstretched towards me, He is saying, 'Come on.' He is drawing closer to me and He is radiant with love. He wants me to come to Him."

"Mother, I don't see anyone standing there."

"He showed me all the things in the past that I've done wrong," she protested. I kept looking in that direction, but did not see Him.

"Oh, but there is someone!" mother assured me.

While the minister was preaching, we went outside and sat on a bench. I explained that the man at the piano was Jesus. I asked mother if she was ready to accept Jesus as her personal Savior. She was more than ready. In reverence, she put her head down. She began to weep more and repented of her sins and asked God to forgive her for hurting people. As the tears continued to flow, she said that she wanted to serve the living God, not Buddha. What a miracle! Mother could not understand a word of English, yet the Holy Spirit lovingly convicted her, and Jesus appeared to her. Mother's life became brand-new after she accepted the Lord.

One day mother received a letter from Korea telling her that Hung Mo was quite ill. The family there urged her to return home because it appeared he was dying. I wondered what we were going to do. We had no money for the trip. Even though our immediate needs were being met, I wanted mother to be able to go to Korea to be with her dying son. At work, I went into a toilet stall and prayed for God to help us. We did not have the necessary thousand dollars to fly mother overseas.

When I came out, a fellow worker asked why I was crying. I told her that I was in prayer for mother and I shared our great need with her. I was amazed when she offered to give me $200.00. A friend from home learned of our need and gave me $300.00. The following Sunday, I testified to the people about the $500.00 that had been given me. After the service, a woman came up to me and handed me an additional $300.00! I was ecstatic! When a Korean pastor I knew found out how the Lord was providing through others, he suggested that I share the good news at his church. He took up an offering which totalled $130.00! Then a man who was able to purchase flights at a discount offered to buy a ticket for mother at a low rate. By doing so, he saved me $70.00.

Mother had seen my prayers answered by this living God, Jesus, and now He had performed this miracle especially for her! Mother went to Korea and spent time with Hung Mo who grew stronger. After his health returned, Mother flew back to the States. We were truly grateful for all that God had done.

Jody in eighth grade.

12

Not a Fighter, But a Lover

A very sweet family lived close to us. Bill and Ruby had two darling boys who were the same ages as Jody and TeJay. The boys played together and got along so well.

I admired Ruby because she seemed to be the perfect homemaker. Ruby was such a hard worker, tended to the yard and flowers, took good care of her boys, kept a clean house, and had hot meals prepared for her husband. I desired to be able to stay home with my boys and be domestic like her, but I had to work while mother tended the house and watched the kids.

Before Jerry moved out, mother told me that he would go over to Ruby's and visit with her. Since we had no phone, I figured he needed to use theirs. Mother was suspicious because Bill worked during the day. I did not think much about it. They were good neighbors and we would go back and forth to each others' homes.

Since the kids played together, I spent a lot of time with Ruby and sometimes I talked to her about the Lord. I knew that she used to be a Christian, and had been raised in a good church, but her love for God had waxed cold and she had lost all desire to serve Him. I did not let her feelings stop me from talking to her about Him.

This relationship developed during the period of time when Jerry and I were separated. I did not know why he wanted to be apart from me, but I knew he desired some time and space for himself.

One day I went out to talk to Ruby, but she seemed so distant. She was aware of our separation and inquired whether or not Jerry and I were going to get a divorce. "We are separated," I replied, "but I believe God will bring him back."

Ruby asked with a dubious look in her eyes, "Do you really think Jerry will come back to you?"

"Yes, I really do," I answered confidently. "I am not worried about it."

"I don't think he's going to come back to you," she advised. "How can you accept him after all he's done? The situation doesn't look too hopeful to me, Sun."

Another day when we were visiting in her home, Ruby told me that she had asked Bill for a divorce, but he would not agree to it. Trusting God to mend my marriage, I ministered to Ruby. I told her how God had answered many prayers and that I trusted Him in my marriage.

Ruby became very annoyed with me and said in a cold tone, "This talk makes me very uncomfortable. I don't want to discuss the matter any more. Please, quit talking about God. Just leave. I'm tired!"

"Ruby, I care and I'm very concerned about you."

"Please leave," she repeated. "I don't want to discuss it any further."

I persisted, even following Ruby, who went into the bathroom and closed the door. Standing at the bathroom door, I asked her if I could do anything to help her. Again, she told me to leave.

"Ruby, I'm sorry for bothering you, but I love you and want to be of help," I said right before I left.

With her on my heart and mind, I prayed and prayed. Within a half hour, she came to my house. She said, "I want to talk to you, alone. I don't want the kids to hear."

"What is this about?" I inquired.

"Meet me at McDonald's tomorrow at noon."

"OK," I agreed. After she left, I could not stand the suspense. I just had to know. I did not want to wait till the next day. I walked over to her house.
"Ruby, please tell me *now*."

"No! My husband and boys are here. We have to wait," she repeated.

Her secrecy caused me to wonder if mother's suspicions had been true. Later that evening, I walked back over because her husband had pulled out of the driveway and the boys were playing outside. Walking into the living room, I said, "Ruby, don't drag it out any longer. I feel that I know what you want to tell me."

She began to cry. "Jerry made a pass at me. He constantly told me he was in love with me," she explained through her tears.

"Oh, Ruby," I sighed, "Is that why you asked Bill for a divorce?"

"Yes," she replied.

"Do you love my husband?" I inquired.

"Yes, Sun. And I know he loves me."

God poured His grace upon me to enable me to handle this situation. Ruby broke down and I put my arms around her. I should have been the one being comforted, but I found myself comforting Ruby.

"Ruby, everything will work out. I forgive you and I love you. Don't worry. I'm not angry with you." She responded with a hug. I left for home, realizing why God placed the need to pray for her so heavily on my heart, causing me to talk to her about the Lord.

God had taken the anger, bitterness and rejection from my life and replaced it with His love and forgiveness. For once, I was not thinking of revenge. Great joy overwhelmed me as I realized I was no longer a fighter, but a lover.

A week later, Ruby asked me to help her find a job. She was thinking ahead, wanting to leave Bill and support herself. I drove her to Indianapolis to help her submit applications to various places. I wanted to take advantage of the opportunity of being together to share more of the Lord with her.

"Ruby, you need the Lord in your life. People think He's just a crutch for the weak, but they don't really understand. We all face problems in life, but those who serve the Lord have answers and added strength. God isn't a crutch; He's the answer to life."

Ruby stiffened as I continued my witness. "Some expect Christians to be perfect and do no wrong, but we have problems and face tough times like everyone else.

We have hope and God picks us up when we slip and fall. He is faithful during our times of need. You know, Ruby, all of mankind is needy and weak. We all have need of God to fill the inner vacuum within each of us, but so many choose to live their own life- style and forget God. What people don't realize is that He wants to give us a full, satisfying life with peace and joy that money can't buy."

I was not sure whether Ruby was receiving what I was saying, but I continued, "Just as a rebellious son returns to his parents who receive him back in their arms, so does God. He cherishes the return of His rebellious children. He wants a personal relationship with each of us."

"Sun, I used to attend a good church, " Ruby admitted, "but I didn't seem to get much out of it, because I saw all the hypocrites."

I responded to her concern by saying, "I will say this. If a person wants to lead his life without God, then God will allow that. He will never force His will on any of us. Some people are deceived into believing that God is cruel for sending people to hell. What they don't know is that hell wasn't created for man, but for the devil and his imps. Man has the free choice to decide where he will spend eternity. God grants man that option. God says that He desires for no man to perish. The important thing is the relationship people have with their Father God. His love for us is greater than a mother's love for her child."

With a defensive tone in her voice, Ruby spoke up, "Jerry loves me and told me that he doesn't love you any more. It may be hard for you to accept, but it's true."

Astonished, I asked, "Do you really believe that Jerry and I will get a divorce?"

Ruby answered with a question, "How do you think you can live with a man who has no love for you?"

I began to wonder if she had blocked out everything I said to her. There was a lot of silence as we drove along. Ruby seemed to be thinking about what I shared with her, but she felt it was safer to hold onto the reins of her life. She did not believe God wanted only the best for her and her husband.

Jerry was not aware that Ruby and I had talked. He tried to keep his plans secret. During the day, he called Ruby, who refused to answer. She let the phone ring off the hook because her conscience was beginning to bother her. Jerry certainly did not want to take any risks by driving to her house, because mother or one of the boys might possibly see him.

Since Jerry had difficulty contacting Ruby, he started coming over to see us. He hoped this would give him an opportunity to learn what was happening. Six weeks after Jerry left me, I admitted to him that I was aware of his love for Ruby. "Do you believe everything you hear, Sun? It's not true," Jerry lied.

I refused to press the issue with him any further. All his lies made it seem so hopeless.

One Saturday morning, when Jerry came to spend some time with me and the boys, we heard a knock on the door. It was Bill standing at the door drunk. He said, "Jerry, my wife wants to talk to you about something." Jerry gave me a funny look, and asked me what he should do. "Go ahead and talk to her," I responded. Bill and Jerry walked back to his house to see Ruby.

As soon as they entered Bill's garage, Bill grabbed a chain and began beating Jerry with it. Jerry was unable to defend himself as Bill continued swinging the chain. Jerry fell over with blood gushing from his head. His knees were also bleeding from the fall, but Bill continued.

Ruby peered out and saw the horrid sight. She began screaming and cursing Bill to stop his mad beating. Finally, Bill let up and Jerry limped towards our house. When he entered the house, bleeding and sore, I asked what happened. I assumed Bill had vented his anger against Jerry.

"Bill got mad and beat me up for no reason," Jerry lied.

"He beat you for no reason at all?" I asked.

"That man is crazy. He's drunk and doesn't know what he's doing," Jerry trembled. Soon he broke down and cried, "You were right all along, honey. Bill is furious with me for spending time with Ruby."

"I'm so sorry, honey. I really do want to come home and be with my family. Honey, will you take me back?" my husband asked.

"Yes, Jerry, you may come home whenever you're ready," I agreed. It was humorous that Jerry had received his just punishment, but I kept my giggle within and showed him much compassion, as the Lord would have done. I said nothing more. He had been through enough that day.

Later, Ruby told me that Bill had been out looking for Jerry on the night before the beating, but could not find him. So Bill went out drinking. The next morning, Bill knew that Jerry was at home with me and came to get even. Why Bill never shot Jerry after finding him, I do not know.

Tejay in sixth grade.

13

God, I Give Up!

Even though Jerry was back at home, our financial struggles continued. People threatened to sue us if we did not pay our bills. I was doing all I knew to do.

The pressure was so heavy on us that Jerry became extremely nervous and smoked four packs of cigarettes a day. He drank in bars. He told me that he did not want to drink and smoke, but he could not control himself. There were times when he would take off for two or three days. He was unsettled and restless.

One day he said he did not want a job; he did not want a family or the responsibility. He was confused and double-minded. Another time, he informed me that he wanted to quit his job and become a truck driver — to drive around, get away and see the different sights.

I said, "Honey, it's too late to get out of your responsibilities. Like it or not, you do have a family to provide for. You can't leave your job whenever you fancy and get another one. Besides, we aren't meeting our bills now. How in the world are you going to pay for a truck? I don't understand." Jerry kept pushing me with the same issue day after day. He was very troubled.

I knew he was seeing other women again. He transmitted diseases to me, and continued to stray. I wondered how much more I could take. I continued to forgive Jerry, but there had to be a limit.

We both agreed on one thing. We had to sell the house. Bills had to be paid or else we would be sued. We put a "For Sale" sign up in the yard. December of 1978 was a difficult time to sell the house, with inflation running rampant and lay-offs occurring regularly in the factories.

I prayed, "Lord, if it's your will, then please help us sell the house with some profit to pay off some things. I would love to live in a new place when the new year begins."

One month later, in answer to prayer, the house was sold! It was January, 1979. After the house was sold, Jerry left us and rented an apartment in Indianapolis. He wanted nothing to do with God and neglected his family responsibilities.

I wanted Jerry to stay with us, but I was not going to fight him. If he did not want to stay with us, then I would not force him. Mother, the boys and I rented a house in Greenfield.

I was able to get a factory job in this small Indiana town, but it did not provide much income. At work, someone suggested that I get food stamps at the welfare office.

I followed through with this suggestion and I shared part of my story with one of the social workers. I told her that my coming to the office was the last thing I wanted to resort to, but I had to do something. She was very comforting and sweet, even radiant when she smiled.

While talking, she told me about the church she was attending and asked me to visit there. I had been visiting a number of churches since our move, but was not at home in any of them. She told me about the beautiful ways in which the Lord moved and touched people's lives. One Sunday I went to her church. The people were very loving and accepting of me. They freely praised the Lord; some stood, some sat, but all worshiped the Lord in their own way. It was a precious meeting.

In May, 1979, my sister Ann and her family came to the States to live. Three years previously, I had invited them to live over here, but the immigration paperwork took a long time to be completed. Before my brother-in-law arrived, someone had lined up a job for him.

None of them could speak English, and they could not drive a car. Ann, her husband and three children lived with us in our little rented home for a week. Then they moved into their own place.

Much to my relief, a Korean pastor came to me and told me of a year-old factory in Indianapolis. He told me that the factory was in need of workers. Since we always needed more money, Ann, Mother, and I began working there. Another Korean lady, Chang from Indianapolis, worked along with us. I was the only one of the four Koreans who could speak English. I was the leader in our small group. They received their instructions from me. I told them how to make the tools. I had never held a position of authority until that job.

For two weeks, the four of us worked diligently. The American workers praised our good work. We desperately needed our jobs, so we worked our best to keep our positions.

One day, as we toiled in the summer heat, my mother became sick. We figured she was worn out from working too hard in the heat. The following day, mother could not talk and her eyes rolled up in their sockets. The right side of her body became paralyzed. The doctor informed us that she had had a stroke.

For a while, I was run ragged. I took my sister to and from work. We would work eight hours, then I would prepare Korean food for mother, who could not eat American food, and take it to the hospital. In addition, I had to tend to the house and kids. I was exhausted.

Mother remained in the hospital for a week. Three weeks after her stroke, Jerry came to see me. He wanted me to consider getting back together. I told him that I would give it some thought while he was away for a couple weeks attending summer camp with the National Guard.

The next Saturday one of his buddies came to my place to tell me that Jerry had been in the hospital. "He wanted me to tell you that ever since Wednesday, he's been having chest pains. By Friday, he was doing fine. The doctors couldn't find anything wrong. Now he's resting in the barracks. He's doing fine now, but wanted you to know that he was not well."

I was rather surprised to hear this because Jerry had always been a very strong, healthy man. I knew he had been very nervous and hyper — maybe that had caused his problem.

On Sunday night, I got a call from someone telling me that Jerry had had a massive heart attack. All his vital signs had ceased for eight minutes and then he was resuscitated. The man who called told me to come to the hospital as soon as possible.

Immediately, I contacted Jerry's mother, who was living with one of her sons. Jerry's father had died from a heart attack a couple of years before. Jerry's brother, Dennis, and his sister-in-law, Jackie, drove to Greenfield with mom. I called Pastor Lee, a Korean minister, to join us because I was nervous and upset. Pastor Lee and I followed Jerry's family as we drove to the hospital in Columbus, Indiana.

Pastor Lee and I prayed on the way. I told him that I had prayed three years for Jerry's salvation and that I believed he would come to know God deeply. I wanted the two of us to serve the Lord together and be one in the Spirit.

"Pastor Lee, isn't God going to grant my request?" I asked. Comfortingly Pastor Lee said, "Surely God will faithfully answer your prayer. I trust that He will give you the assurance you need."

As we walked into the hospital room, my mind went wild with all kinds of frightening thoughts. A machine was keeping Jerry's heart pumping. The doctor gave us no encouraging words because Jerry was unconscious.

Pastor Lee and I laid our hands on Jerry. I prayed, "Give him a new life and bind our marriage together. Lord, you know all things, and see every man's soul. If

Jerry's health doesn't improve, then please give me the assurance that he will be with you."

While Jerry's family and I were in the hospital room, I felt very uncomfortable. They were not warm and sweet to me. I felt that they were blaming me for Jerry's poor health. For a while there was silence until Jerry's mother spoke up, "If Jerry remains sick I will take care of him. I will get his car and furniture, too."

"Mom, we can discuss it when Jerry is conscious," I said.

Angrily, she yelled at me in front of the others, "You and Jerry aren't even living together. You aren't family any more."

"I didn't ask for the separation," I said. "He walked out on me." My words went in one ear and out the other.

That same week, I received notice that I had to go to the Richmond, Indiana, Courthouse. There were some things that had to be settled legally, because Jerry and I had filed for bankruptcy a few months earlier. My lawyer, and a good friend of mine, went with me to Richmond.

My lawyer, Sonya, and I entered a room and faced the judge and five other people who wanted payments from me. The judge questioned, "Can you make your payments to these people?"

"No, sir. I can't," I replied.

"What do you intend to do?" he asked sternly.

I had no choice except to give permission for the return of the items which I bought on credit back to the creditors.

In a hallway at the courthouse, I found a bench and sat down for a good cry. "God, what I going to do?"

All of a sudden the Lord spoke to me, *"Let go."* He reminded me of the Scripture that says, "If anyone does not give up all he has, he cannot be His disciple." (Luke 14:33).

For the three years I had been serving God, I had not fully released myself, my loved ones and all my belongings to Him. "Alright, Lord," I said, as I handed Him the unseen belongings. "I surrender mother, Jerry, the boys and every other family member into your care. You tell us in First Peter 5:7 to cast all our cares on you for you care for us. I give all my cares and burdens to you. I give you my house, the furniture, my job, my finances..." I released everyone and everything I could think of.

After a good cry, I felt relieved inside. I did not feel the stress and strain I felt earlier. The heaviness was gone and I felt light all over. I also felt comforted, knowing that I had God to rely on. He would never leave me, nor forsake me, so I began rejoicing. Before we left Richmond, I found out that the creditors decided not to repossess the furniture. God had proved that He cares for me.

The next evening, four nights after the heart attack, Jerry regained consciousness. A nurse told me that he asked for me. His mom resented the fact that he did not ask for her. Her attitude towards me was very upsetting, but there was nothing I could do.

As I walked into Jerry's room, I was so relieved to see him awake. "Honey," I said softly. "Did you know what happened to you? You had a massive heart attack and actually died for a few minutes. You've been unconscious for four days."

He answered, "I can't remember a thing. All I know is that I fell backwards."

"Yes," I replied. "The doctor said you hurt the back of your head from falling on the cement. Oh, I'm so thankful you're awake and talking and that your life was spared."

"Honey, it is so good to see you," Jerry smiled.

"Your family is in the waiting room. We can only come in one at a time. You certainly gave everybody quite a scare," I said. For a few moments, we looked at each other as I held his hand and stroked his arm.

Jerry and I spent some time talking, and he was so sorry for all the grief he had caused in my life. He was full of remorse for neglecting his family duties and being unfaithful. My heart broke when I heard him talk. I asked if he was ready to stop running from God. With tears welling up in his eyes, he nodded and asked me to pray with him. After experiencing this close brush with death, Jerry surrendered his life to God. Finally, I had the assurance I needed; Jerry had made his peace with the Lord.

"Honey," Jerry spoke. "Do you remember me asking you to think about my moving back in with you and the boys after National Guard camp?"

"Most definitely," I said with my heart pounding.

"Will you let me come back after I get out of here?" he asked hopefully.

"Oh, yes!" I answered with joy. "You can do whatever you want. You can have whatever you want. It will be great to have you home again. You just take care of yourself and get better. The door at home is always open to you, honey!"

His face beamed with a big smile and his eyes sparkled. "Jerry, I'm so happy that you can remember, because the doctor said that if you ever remembered anything it would be a miracle, because your fall on the cement injured your head severely." Jerry had received two miracles that night —healing of his mind and his soul.

After I left the room to visit with the family, they informed me that they had driven Jerry's car back to New Castle. No one had offered to ask me. They had completely erased me from their family.

Mom added, "Sun, by the time Jerry is released from the hospital, he is going to need round-the-clock care. I plan to take him home with me."

"Mom, we aren't divorced — only separated," I reminded her. "Let's wait and discuss all this later."

The family was really getting to me. They had no right to make these decisions without discussing them with Jerry and me. I told mom to allow Jerry the freedom to decide where he wanted to live. She became very upset with me for standing up to her. She always became angry and defensive whenever her control was threatened.

I ran to the restroom and cried. I knew that any little upset could trigger a heart attack, so I wanted no family squabbles or problems to confront my husband.

After I came out of the bathroom, my brother-in-law, Dennis, suggested that the two of us go outside and talk. Sitting at a small table, Dennis asked,
"What is your problem?"

"Dennis, can't you see what your mother is doing to me?" I asked.

In amazement he answered, "I don't see what in the world mother is doing to harm you. She is your husband's mother and she loves Jerry. She just wants to be with him. The doctor told us that Jerry is not going to be able to do anything for a long time. His heart condition is the same as that of a ninety-year-old man. Jerry is going to have a strict diet and constant care. Since dad had a bad heart and mom took good care of him for five years, she knows what to do."

"I don't mind that at all. If that's what Jerry wants, fine. We've been separated and I know what it's like being without him. It's just that Jerry asked to come home with me. I feel *he* must decide, not his family." I continued, "When Jerry was healthy, he walked out on me. I couldn't reject the man I loved then; and now, with him so sick and in need of twenty-four-hour-a-day care, I cannot turn my back on him. I wanted him when he was healthy, and I want him now, even though he is a very sick man. I would like to add that I do not appreciate your family moving his car back to New Castle. Now you want my key to his apartment to get his furniture to take to New Castle, too. Dennis, just what do you expect me to say to Jerry? You and your family are making decisions which are contrary to his wishes. This isn't good. He can't handle any unnecessary stress or strain."

"Well," Dennis said firmly, "I suggest you simply comfort him and leave the rest to us. You just go along with our plans."

Anger rose up from within me and I blurted out, "You know, your family has always hurt me! I've always been a black sheep to this family. I have not done a thing against any of you. I have tried so hard to please Jerry and to be a part of this family, but my efforts have been useless. You are aware of the fact that Jerry ran around with other women and I always took him back!"

"Now, now Sun," Dennis said, as he tried to pacify me. "Don't forget that you came from a poor family in a poor country. You didn't have a thing when Jerry brought you to the States. Now that you have what you want, you should not talk like that."

"Just one minute!" I raised my voice in reply. "Let me inform you of something you may not be aware of. There was a time when Jerry and I had no milk and we were out of groceries. I sent Jerry to ask mom for $20.00. We were in great need. The kids were hungry and mom told Jerry that she didn't have $20.00. She refused to help her son. I actually heard Jerry say he hated her. Your family never helped us when we were hungry, but church people brought us sacks of food.

"When your dad passed away, before she moved in with you, remember the time she divided the furniture from her home between you and Al's family? She gave nothing to us. I have been very patient and have suffered inside. Now, my husband is dying and this family is still rejecting me."

"Come on, Sun. Listen to me. You have more now than what you had in Korea. Do you honestly think you'd have more in Korea?" Dennis asked. I could not answer these questions.

"Sun," Dennis continued. "You just need to be understanding of our family. I didn't know you had been through so much without the food and money. Probably mom had grown tired of Jerry continually borrowing money from her. He'd use it on booze and cigarettes. How was mom to know when you were in dire need? I'm sure she would have helped you if she knew the truth. Just be careful around mom. She's upset enough."

Before long, Jerry was out of intensive care. The family and I were not driving to Columbus each day since he was not so critical. We were like ships in the night passing by; we did not see each other for a couple weeks.

During one visit Jerry said, "Honey, I want you to know that I love you and care for you. I don't want to be a burden to you. Since mom took care of dad because of his heart condition, it's no problem for her to help me through this setback.

"You see, while she's been living with Dennis and Jackie, she's been causing some problems. For everyone involved, it might be best if mom and I rented a place together in New Castle. I'll have insurance and disability checks coming in to help us out. In this way Dennis and Jackie will have some relief, and mom really needs her own place.

"You won't have to tend to another family burden. You don't have four arms and you've been taking care of your mother, too. You have the boys to think of, plus your job. Honey, I'll be able to give you money from these checks which will most likely be more than my employment checks."

I wondered if he really meant it, so I asked, "Is that what you really want?"

He responded only with a pensive look.

Again, I asked, "Is that what you really want?"

Jerry then started to weep, "I really do want you, honey. I really do! I want to go home with you so much, but I'm confused. I just don't know what to do."

Then I knew! The family had already talked to him and persuaded him to change his mind. Jerry was stuck between a rock and a hard place, trying to please me and his family. Jerry was afraid to hurt his controlling, domineering mother. He wanted to keep peace in the family.

"Alright, Jerry," I said, giving in, "I'm with you. No matter what you decide, I'll go along with you. I love you. All I care about is for you to get better. If there's someone better than me to nurse you back to health, then go with that one."

Late that night, the phone rang at home. Jackie called to further discuss arrangements concerning Jerry. "Hi, Sun. Have you seen Jerry lately?"

"Yes," I replied. "As a matter of fact, I just returned from seeing him a little while ago."

"Did he tell you about his plans when he gets out?"

I told her what Jerry planned to do.

"Well, Sun, don't you think that's best for him and Mom?"

Unknown to me, Dennis and Jackie's motive was to get rid of Mom, who had been trying to control their family life. They tried to fool me into believing that they were intending to help me out, as well as Mom and Jerry.

"Jackie, I'd like to know what's going on. Jerry told me his plans, but he says he wants to stay with me. He cried and said he was confused. I'm a bit confused myself."

Jackie explained, "I'll try to be a bit more specific with you. We both know how active Jerry was with other women. Physically, you must remember that his desires remain. You two are young and the risk is too high if anything were to happen to him. You wouldn't want that responsibility, now, would you?"

Jackie had succeeded in convincing me that her ploy was the right thing to do. "I guess you're right," I conceded. "I see what you're saying."

She ended the conversation, "Sun, in the long run, I believe your life will be better."

After we hung up, I was gripped with fear that I'd be the one to blame if anything happened to Jerry under my supervision. Being so confused and fearful, I went to God and asked for His direction. "Lord, what am I to do? You heard what his family had said to me and you know how confused Jerry and I are. What should I do?"

The Lord spoke to my heart to let go of the situation and give Him the care. He did not want me to carry the burden, but to trust Him to take care of it.

"Alright, Lord. I give the care to you. If Jerry comes home with me, fine. If he lives with Mom that's fine, too. You work it out." I decided to rest in the truth of Jeremiah 33:3: "Call to me and I will answer you and tell you great and unsearchable things you do not know."

Nearly a month had passed since the heart attack, and while I visited Jerry one Sunday afternoon he said, "Do you want to hear some great news? It sounds like I'm going to get to leave this place in three days."

"That's wonderful news, Jerry!"

"There's no need for you to come back all this way any more because I could even get out tomorrow. I'm not certain. I'll call you before I leave. So stay home until you hear from me."

Three days later, on Wednesday night, Jerry called me. "Hi, honey! Guess where I am?"

"Where?"

"I'm home now!"

"What?!" I asked as my heart sank. He was supposed to call me before he left the hospital to let me know whether I was to pick him up or to contact his mother.

"How long have you been home, Jerry?"

"For two days," he answered.

"For two days?" I asked with surprise in my voice.

"Yeah, I wanted to let you know that I've decided to stay with Mom. She's been looking for a place to rent, and the way it looks now, Mom and I may move next weekend.

"There's something else I want to tell you. I've been selfish with you, and I feel that I need to let you be free. You won't have much of a marriage being married to me any more."

I was crushed as he continued, "Besides, with Mom overseeing me and my checking and savings accounts, we need to make some changes. Legally, you have the authority to endorse my checks, but we need to give Mom the authority now.

"This will help you out, too — I'll send you money, too. Don't worry about the support check once everything is settled."

Unknown to me, Jerry would be receiving sizable checks for his disability from the insurance company, which would fully support Jerry and his mother. All I cared about, however, was his health and his soul.

"OK, honey, whatever you want," I said, completely stunned. After we hung up, I cried and cried. Rejection struck an ugly chord in my heart once more. How had his family changed his mind? He had said he wanted to be at home with the children and me. My heart grieved to know that Jerry's life had changed and we would not be together any more. I refused to fight the divorce because I did not want to make a scene with the family and risk injuring Jerry's health even more. His family might have thought that I was out to get more money, which was not the case. I could not be able to bear the blame if Jerry grew worse or died.

All in all, I did not want the divorce and I did not believe Jerry did either, but his family's influence was too great to fight.

I went to my Refuge and asked, "Lord, why does this have to happen? Now that I have a man with a heart after God, he wants to end the marriage. I have the kind of man I've always wanted, yet now I have to give him up. Why? You know my heart and you see that it's breaking."

He reminded me that I had committed the whole decision to Him. "Okay, Lord. I told you I'd accept whatever happens." I knew I had to trust Him because He had always worked things out in my life. Two days later, on August 9, 1979, I went before a judge, raising my hand as he spoke. I signed some papers and walked out of the courthouse as a divorced woman.

TeJay's birthday was the next day, so the boys and I drove to New Castle to see Jerry and celebrate. The rest of the family was outside on the porch. This gave us some privacy.

When I saw Jerry, he looked very pale and weak. He wanted me to sit on his lap, but I was very hesitant. After he insisted, I gave in. He hugged me and apologized again for all the things he did to hurt me.

Jerry said, "Honey, I will never hurt you again. I love you so much. You are so beautiful. What you did yesterday was for the best. I can't hold you back. You are free to marry anyone, now. Whether or not you ever have another man in your life, please come and bring the boys. We can always remain friends.

"The doctor even mentioned the possibility of a heart transplant. If that's successful we could consider remarriage if you desire to. If anything happens to me, you're too young to stay single. I want you to remarry if you ever have the opportunity."

I was amazed at how sweet and loving he was to me. Ironically, with the marriage over, he was completely different towards me. Jerry was very loving and kind.

"By the way, sweetie. I have some money to give you. With checks coming in, I want to help you out. Mom hid the money in the freezer. We put money back for the deposit and the rent for our apartment, which we plan to move into next week. I know we have extra."

We walked to the freezer. After he opened it, he rummaged around looking for the hidden cash, but could not find it. "It's gone," Jerry said in an alarmed tone. "Someone moved it. I saw Mom put it there. I told her that I needed some money to give to you and the boys."

Opening his billfold to give me money, I saw tears in his eyes. There was only $7.00. "Honey, I'm so sorry. I wanted to give you at least $50.00, but this is all I have. I'll ask Mom."

"No, Jerry, don't bother! I figure she moved the money because you wanted to give me some. Forget it. Don't even ask."

Before I left, Jerry told me to call him on the following Friday. He felt it would be more convenient for me to call since I worked.

"I can come and see you each day," I replied.

"Oh, no, Sun. Just come once a week. You have far too much to do with your job and the boys and your mom to tend to," he said lovingly.

After a week had passed, I called on Friday evening. Mom answered. I asked to talk to Jerry. "No, you can't," she said.

"Why not?" I asked.

"He isn't here. He's been in the hospital since Sunday afternoon. He had another heart attack," she snapped.

No one had contacted me. I assumed he was getting the proper care and that I would have been informed if there was a problem. I asked why no one had called me.

"We tried to call you," Mom curtly replied. "No one could get ahold of you."

"You could have given mother a message. She is always there. The boys can take messages, too," I pointed out.

"Well, no one answered," she snapped again.

"Mom, I want to see Jerry," I finally said.

"You can't see him! Only family is allowed to visit. You aren't family any more. I saw in the newspaper that you two are divorced. I didn't know you were going to get a divorce. That shocked Jerry," she said.

Mom had no idea how deeply she had hurt me. "How bad is Jerry?" I asked.

Mom said cheerfully, "Oh, he's getting better."

"Really?" I asked. "I want to see him and I know he wants to see me," I insisted.

"If he wants to see you, I'm not aware of it," she said.

I begged, "Mom, please let me see him."

She coldly informed me, "Only family is allowed to see him every four hours for ten minutes. We all take turns. I don't know when you can see him."

"How about early in the morning?" I suggested.

"That's when one of us goes to see him," she said, continuing to argue with me.

"How about midnight?" I suggested again.

"We need to let him rest. No one should be allowed to see him at that hour," she barked. Finally we agreed that I could see him at 6:00 the following morning.

That night, I set my alarm for 5:00 am. Unfortunately, it did not go off. I woke up at 6:00 am and I knew I'd never make it in time. I felt sick inside.

On the morning of August 18, 1979, I took mother and the boys to stay with my sister Ann. It was very unusual for the boys to want to go to her house because they did not understand Korean. I relished the time alone when I got home. I received a phone call from a friend who said she and some other friends wanted to drop over in the evening to see me. I thought the company would do me good.

Around four o'clock in the afternoon I decided to clean. As I dusted the furniture in the boys' room, I longed for Jerry desperately. I missed him so much, and love welled up so strongly in me that I felt I could have died for him. Never before had I felt such a tremendous love for him. I recalled the time we bought the bed in the room I was cleaning and beautiful memories of the two of us together began to overwhelm me.

I spotted an album which he loved, so I put it on the stereo and played its contemporary Christian music. I cried and cried and cried. He was so strong within my heart. I regretted that I had not brought him home. I yearned for him so much that I literally hurt inside.

Then I prayed and told God I could not handle my feelings for Jerry. "Take this heaviness off of me. I release Jerry to you," and I raised my hands to Him as if I were literally surrendering Jerry. Immediately the burden lifted. I thought Jerry must be doing better. As the clock chimed six, I felt relieved and comforted.

About a half-hour later, my friends arrived. I shared with them what I had been going through that afternoon as we ate pizza together.

At 9:30 pm, Jerry's younger brother Al called to tell me that Jerry had died a few minutes after six o'clock that evening. That was the exact time when my heavy burden for Jerry had lifted.

I let out a scream. Why was I not informed of his death earlier, I wondered. I became hysterical. Dropping the phone I yelled, "It's my fault —it's my fault. I let him go."

My girl friend grabbed me and said, "Get ahold of yourself! You have no authority over life or death. Only God had that authority. Who do you think you are to believe you killed him? How could you have killed the man?

"Just think how God protected you through all this. If he would've come home with you and then died, not only would you blame yourself, but Jerry's family would probably hold you responsible. Knowing that, you would have most likely gone stark, raving mad!"

Another friend grabbed the phone. Al said, "Tell Sun that she needs to come to New Castle tomorrow to sign some papers. All of Jerry's benefits are in her name."

Mom's ploy had backfired. Eventually, Jerry would have made the proper changes, but he never got around to it. I was responsible for the funeral arrangements, as well.

I learned later that Jerry told his mother four hours before his death that he was going home that day. Later we realized he had meant heaven. About four o'clock, he went into a coma, dying shortly after six o'clock in the evening. I understood why I felt such a burden for him at the time he went into a coma; and right before his death, I felt a release and a calm that everything would be all right.

God ministered to me before he died and I had a healing of my memories in which all I could remember were the good times of our marriage.

Tony Fannin (Sun's stepson) senior picture 1980.

Top Row (L. to R.): Sun, Larry, Jody, two of
Dr. Choi's assistants.
Bottom Row: (L. to R.) Tejay, Dr. Choi, Mama Lee.

14

God Gives the Desires of My Heart

Two weeks after Jerry's death, Larry Fannin, an old friend, dropped by to see the boys and me. Larry, Loti, Jerry and I had been friends. Larry and I were always trying to win our mates to the Lord; however, both marriages had ended in divorce. Larry and Loti had been divorced for five months. Larry wanted to take the three of us to a movie. Since I was expecting some friends over from the Korean church, Larry and the two boys went on.

Around ten o'clock, they returned. Pastor Lee began to visit with Larry. "Are you still an elder at your church in New Castle?" he inquired. "I know you've been very active."

"No," Larry responded. "Since the divorce, I resigned from the leadership. I know I hurt some people and I feel like I've lost a lot of people's respect. I used to teach, but after the divorce many lost their confidence in me. It hurt me terribly — more than anyone knows. So, I left. I've been going to church in Muncie."

"How do you like it?" Pastor Lee continued.

"Well, it's nice, but nothing like the one I left. It's one of those things that happened. I can't go back knowing I hurt people. It tears me up to think about it — some people don't want anything to do with me."

Pastor Lee made a proposal, "Larry, what do you think about coming to our Korean church? You preach, and Sun can interpret. I've prayed for seven years for an American man to preach because most of the congregation is made up of American men who are married to Korean women. In this way you can minister to the men, and while Sun interprets your messages, she'll be ministering to the women.

"I want to see the families worshipping together. What I've seen is the frustration that the men go through because they don't understand Korean, and yet the women are frustrated in an American church. I have such a burden for these people. Here, before my very eyes, I see the answer to my prayer. I have no doubt that God is going to use you two."

"Well, Pastor Lee," Larry replied, "Give me a couple weeks to pray about it and then I'll give you an answer. You pray about it, too."

Larry knew the Lord had a calling on his life. Although he had been through a divorce, he was not going to give up and quit. People may reject and throw out divorcees, but God does not do that. God cleanses and forgets our mistakes and failures; then we continue onward to better changes.

Both Larry and I were in agreement about teaching at the Korean church. For other services we attended American churches in the community together. On Wednesdays before church, Larry came to my home early so we could study and prepare for the Korean services on Sunday afternoons. We ministered there for about four and half months.

During this time, a month after Jerry's death, I had a dream. In the dream, a man appeared to me and told me that he wanted to marry me. I could not identify the man. I quickly responded, "No! I'm not going to marry you!" I was doing fine without a man in my life and I did not want to go through another hardship as before. I did not mind dating or going out for dinner, but not marriage. Since I was free from men, I was not going to allow myself to be controlled, hurt or hindered in my Christian walk. I had had too many bad experiences.

The man in the dream pressed on and said, "I really believe you're going to marry me."

"No, sir," I said adamantly.

"Instead of saying 'no,' why don't we kneel down and ask God what He would have us to do? Do you know God's will in your life? Have you ever prayed and asked Him?"

Well, I figured it would not hurt to pray, so we did. We prayed for His guidance and direction for our lives. All of a sudden, there was a knock at the door. A couple inquired about what we were doing.

"We're just seeking God's direction."

They asked, "May we join you?" So, the four of us knelt down to pray until there was another knock at the door. A second couple asked the same thing and desired to join us, too. As the time passed on, more and more people came to join us in prayer.

The next thing I saw in the dream was the room packed full of people. "O, God, we don't have enough room in my living room. We need a bigger place." Then I woke up.

As the days passed, after Jerry's life insurance check from his place of employment came to me, it felt so good to finally have my debts paid. As the money accumulated from various sources, I asked the Lord what to do with the extra money, desiring His direction.

One day at work I felt impressed of God to go to Cranberry Lake Estates, north of Greenfield. I thought these homes were too expensive, but I drove there anyway, and spotted a "For Sale" sign in front of a nice home. I was impressed with the size of the house and thought I could have Korean prayer meetings in the large living room. I went back home feeling God wanted this house for my family, but not knowing how it could ever work out. The next day our life insurance man came by with a check. I was totally unaware of the policy, but God had known before when He guided me to see the house in Cranberry Lake Estates. The details of purchases were worked out and our family moved in shortly before Thanksgiving, 1979.

As the months passed, Larry and I continued ministering together. He found that he was falling in love with me. He appreciated how the Lord was using us together so beautifully and thought we made a great team. He began telling me he loved me, but I resisted. I did not feel that I needed a man, and deep down, I did not want to be a disloyal friend to Loti. I saw Larry only as a very special friend. Besides, I was doing great financially. I did not need a man to support me, for I was quite capable of doing it myself.

As Larry continued to bring up the subject of marriage, I would warn him not to get close or involved because I was not planning to marry him.

Gently he would voice his opinion, "Well, Sun, I believe God is putting us together and He's granting us another opportunity to serve Him together. It's been your heart's desire to be one with a man and serve God together."

During the Christmas season of 1979, Larry spent a lot of time with our family. He was just like a part of the family. At this time I noticed I was beginning to love him more than just as a brother in the Lord. He was very respectable, had a good character, but in the back of my mind I still connected Larry with Loti. There was no way I could hurt her. Besides, I was afraid of what people would think — I was bound with the fear of man. I figured that people would think of me as a awful person for marrying my friend's ex-husband.

Larry continued to call and visit and tell me he loved me. "Larry," I said, "Jerry died five months ago and people might think we had something going on between the two of us. That's not too good. I've been accused so much in my life, and I don't want any more accusations." Struggling with my feelings, I stubbornly resisted Larry as he continued to encourage our relationship.

I was miserable inside. I was in a fix between two

opinions. One, I was hurting Larry, who was a beautiful person. And two, I would hurt Loti if I gave in to Larry.

Again, in a dream, the Lord dealt with me. I was one hard nut to crack. I recall driving up a mountain. My goal was to reach the peak. As I drove upwards, I kept slipping back. With my stubborn nature, I was determined to reach the top, so I would keep trying. Then, Larry appeared in the dream. He offered to help push me up.

I said, "No, I can do it myself. I don't need your help."

He replied gently, "You need my help. I need to push you up so you can go."

Again, I refused his help. "No, I can do it myself. Don't bother me, leave me alone." I was behaving like a spoiled child.

"Well, alright, " he said, resigning from assisting me.

I continued in vain to drive up the mountain. No success. Finally I gave up.

"You can help me now," I said to Larry. As he pushed, we spotted a water fountain. We were very thirsty, so we stopped to refresh ourselves. "I'm going up again by myself," I insisted. As I kept slipping, he offered to assist me again. Again I insisted, "No! Leave me alone!"

Gently, yet more sternly, Larry said, "You *need* my help. Let me pull you up." The same thing happened. So I gave up and allowed him to help me.

Once we reached the peak, many people from all over came to us, saying "Where have you guys been? We've been looking for you." I was amazed at the masses who kept inquiring about our whereabouts.

They anxiously told us to pray for them. One by one, as Larry laid hands on people and prayed for them, they fell under the power of God. I had never seen anything like it in my life. After he prayed for all the people, I asked, "How about praying for me?"

As soon as he did, I saw myself fall under the power, too. Then I woke up.

I knew the Lord was speaking loud and clear to me. Finally, I could see that I needed Larry to help me, to push me and pull me up, spiritually. The water represented the Holy Spirit, and I knew that with both of us drinking from the living waters we would be ministering together; Larry would not be a hindrance as Jerry had been, but a help and a supporter to me; we'd be side by side, serving God together.

It was obvious that we had a ministry. The Lord was going to bring the people to us who would receive us. We would not have to go out looking for them.

In February of 1980, Larry and I went to church. Still holding on to my independence, I was crying out to God in misery. He spoke back very clearly, *"I gave you all you've needed. You have desired a husband who would serve Me along with you. What do you want Me to do now that I have granted your request? Why are you not receiving the answer to the petition you have asked?"*

The pastor then called Larry and me up front. He said, "The Lord had a word for you two. He says that He has brought you together to become one in the spirit, one mind, and one flesh."

His word confirmed to me that God truly spoke to me in the dream and that Larry and I were to marry.

I confessed to Larry that I had been more fearful of man than of God. But I now knew beyond a shadow of a doubt that we were to be together. By Korean tradition I had not had a proper mourning period for my late husband. I felt so strongly that God had confirmed this in my heart and I knew that this was His will, so I joyfully chose to serve God rather than man.

On March 22, 1980, Larry and I were married. Larry helped me overcome insecurity by telling me how beautiful I was and that I was intelligent, with the capacity to do anything I set my mind to. He constantly encouraged me by complimenting the good traits in me. Every day, with a hug, he told me he loved me and thanked the Lord for giving me to be his wife. He told me how special and righteous I was before the Lord. He encouraged me in the faith by saying that God had honored my child-like faith. It seemed that everything I did was special to him.

Larry is a beautiful father to the boys. He spends time with them, listening and showing them the love they need. He attends many of their ball games and gets down and wrestles, teases them, and plays with them. They go to movies and have fun times together.

Larry and I found it a touching moment the day we returned from our short honeymoon. The boys came to greet us at the front door, so happy to see us. They asked if they could call Larry their daddy.

Larry is also very good to mother. No matter what she does, he never complains. Larry appreciates her help in the house. This leaves more time for Larry and me to spend together in ministry. Mother is a tremendous help to us. God has healed my mother of the stroke. Larry's family welcomed me with open arms. His parents are precious and loving to me. Finally, I had found the father I had longed for all my life. His sister and her husband are so kind and warm. Larry's son, Tony, accepted me right away and through the years we have grown closer. It did not take long to consider Tony as one of my own sons. I now know I am a part of the family.

For once, I lacked nothing in my life. I had so much joy and happiness. I was abundantly blessed — financially, emotionally, spiritually, in every conceivable way, and my cup was running over. Life could not have been better.

L to R: Larry Fannin, Steve Sampson, and Bob Wakeland
at the Body of Christ Fellowship in Greenfield, Ind.

Mama Lee and Joe Turnbloom.

15

Preparation For Ministry

In May, I had another dream. I saw masses of people excitedly yelling, "Look, look! There's Jesus coming down." I beheld a great number of people behind Him, too. Then I looked and saw unbelievers mocking and scorning, "You're crazy. We don't see anything. That's not Jesus!" Then the believers continued to exclaim, "That's Him —that's Jesus!"

As I watched Jesus descend in all His splendor and glory, the believers fell, face down, to the ground. We were frightened and crying for forgiveness. The sight was very awesome. Then, as I looked up, I saw a gorgeous, rich-looking treasure chest coming down from the sky. It was brimming over with riches and jewels and treasures — all sparkling and glowing. When the believers saw the beauty of this trove they ran to grab it. The jewels fell from the chest, but I was unable to catch any. I saw the jewels and the chest fall into the ocean. I was so disappointed not to have gotten one piece of treasure. Then I awoke.

After praying for three days, I received the interpretation of the dream. In the dream I saw that I was not truly holy within. The ocean which seemed limitless represented God whose love is unlimited. The water represented the Holy Spirit. The treasure represented the blessings and promises from the Bible. As the treasures drifted to the depths of the sea, the Lord showed me that we must dig deep and search in the Word of God for the precious nuggets, as we would search for priceless treasures in the sea.

Matthew 7:7 tells us to "Ask and it shall be given, seek and you shall find; knock and the door shall be opened to you." In my heart, I knew I needed to study and learn the Word. That's seeking and finding. That's where the real treasures in life are found. The treasures are peace, joy, love, prosperity, divine protection, success, direction, health, righteousness. All these blessings could be mine, but I needed more knowledge and understanding.

It would take time, effort, and diligence to accomplish this task. When one finds a jewel, there's a great joy. It's your possession, your rich inheritance. When a student of God's Word discovers a promise to meet a need, there's great joy. It's our inheritance as children of God.

We are told to study to show ourselves approved unto God. Ephesians 5:26 says "...to make her holy, cleansing her by the washing with water through the word" (*NIV*). We are made holy through a cleansing process. What cleansing? By the washing of water by the Word. As people read and meditate on the Word of God there is a

refreshing and a cleansing which occurs within the soul.
The mind becomes renewed, thoughts become clean and
pure, and the individual becomes holy. Holiness does not
stem from our outward appearance: whether we wear
make-up or the type of apparel we wear or from hair
styles and physical adornment. True holiness comes from
within. One's inner self radiates the true, unfading beauty
of a gentle and quiet spirit which is of great worth in
God's sight.

My eyes were opened; I needed to prepare myself for
the Lord, as a bride cleanses and purifies and adorns
herself for her groom. If my spirit and soul feed upon the
manna of God's Word, I become prepared and ready to
meet my King Jesus. After the dream, I experienced an
insatiable hunger and thirst for more of God and His
Word. Larry began to order books and tapes from Dr.
Paul Yonggi Cho, who pastors the world's largest church
in Seoul, Korea. Being in my native language, these
teachings were easier for me to understand than
American teachers. While working, I listened to Dr.
Cho's teachings; at lunchtime, I read my Bible. God was
preparing me. Many people called of God go to
seminaries and Christian schools, but the Holy Spirit was
to be my teacher, as I listened to the tapes and continued
to study God's Word.

One day Larry said, "Our home church in New Castle
is having a revival. An evangelist, a prophet of God, will
be speaking. I know we are to go, Sun, because I'm sure
that the Lord has a special word for us."

"You've got to be kidding, Larry. I can't go back there
now that we're married. No way. What will people think?

Your ex-wife went there and I used to attend when I was married to Jerry. I don't want to face the people who knew the four of us." The fear of man was with me again.

For the whole week, Larry patiently awaited my consent. I knew I was hurting him by not going, but I was scared of people's thoughts and words and reactions. I wanted approval so much and I feared their rejection.

The last night when the evangelist was to be at the church, I decided I would go. I knew how badly Larry desired this. The Lord impressed on me to keep my eyes on Him, and not on people.

It was difficult for me to walk inside. Larry grabbed my hand, as we walked to the front and sat down. All the while, he held my hand tightly in his and I kept my head down. I felt the people's eyes on me. Near the end of the service, a number of people walked up front for prayer and ministry.

Larry said, "We need to go up front." I responded with fear in my heart, "No! I'm not going up there!"

"Yes you are. You're going with me," he said emphatically.

"No, I'm not, Larry," I said, resisting his tug on my arm.

Sadly, he said "Alright, then we'll go home." When I realized that Larry would be greatly disappointed, I gave in and said, "Okay, I'll go to the front with you." Inside, I knew I was to go up, but I was scared of the people.

Hand in hand, we walked up front. The evangelist came to me and said, "You have been crying and crying in the past. God is healing you and wiping away your tears. God has protected you as one who is in the cleft of a rock. No one could pluck you out. God is anointing your lips to speak for Him."

Pastor Wakeland walked up behind us, laid his hand on our joined hands, and raised them in the air to show his approval and acceptance of our marriage. He gave us his blessing and prayed for us. The congregation applauded, with smiles on their faces. Unknown to me, they supported us, too. I released my emotions in a flood of tears. They seemed to cleanse the fear of man which had crept into my heart once again.

Larry received an encouraging word from the Lord, too. *"My son, when you stepped forth from the pew, you received what you've desired. The anointing I've given you in the past is going to double. The anointing you will walk in will not compare to the anointing you had in the past. I am going to promote you."* The congregation responded with joy at God's word.

After the service was over, people lined up to shake our hands and tell us how much they loved us. Prior to leaving, Pastor Wakeland hugged me and said, "I want you to know, Sun, that you are always welcome in this church. It's your home. I don't want you to ever walk in with your head down. Keep your head up, young lady."

Ever since that night, I have never experienced the fear of man. That evening in September of 1980 will always be so very special to us.

A month later I was praying for the Lord to use me in the ministry. He showed me that I needed to get rid of bitterness and unforgiveness in my heart towards Jerry's family. After Jerry's death, I held a grudge against them for hurting me in the matters which I considered unethical. In the past when we were hungry, they never offered my family any financial help. Now, after Jerry's death, they never inquired concerning the boys' welfare. For a year, I continued to carry these resentments deeply within.

I found making restitution to Jerry's mother a difficult thing to do. The Lord impressed on me to fast for three days. I wondered how I would make it for three days, but I experienced no hunger. I bought a sweet card and apologized for my negative behavior towards her. Before I could mail it, Larry informed me that Mom had called and wanted me to return her call. God had been working; she phoned me on the third day of my fast. I called and said, "Mom, this is Sun, I heard you had called me. Before you say anything, I want to ask for your forgiveness. I'm so sorry for not bringing the boys over and for not keeping in touch. I haven't been as good to you as I should've been." I broke down and cried.

"Well it's not all your fault," Mom apologized. "I've been selfish, too."

We had a good talk and forgave each other. My tears washed away the hurt and pain I had felt for so long. Taking that step of obedience brought a great reward to me. I felt genuine love for Mom and had peace that passed all understanding. I felt a freedom to visit mom and the family which I had never felt before.

My relationships with Ruby and Loti have also been reconciled beautifully. Ruby and Bill are still married and are busily engaged in the raising of their two boys. Loti has remarried. God gave me the privilege of praying with her when she rededicated her life to the Lord.

My relationship with Hung Mo has been healed as well. He has apologized for the abusive way he used to treat me. He asked for my forgiveness, but through God's grace I had forgiven him long before he asked for it. We both love each other very much. Knowing it was Hung Mo's responsibility, he showed great appreciation to Larry and I for giving mother a happy home.

In February of 1981, I had another dream. I found myself beside a river. I was walking along in the sand. I knew I had to cross to the other side of the river, but I could not swim. I asked God for help because there was no boat and no one to assist me. All of a sudden, Jesus appeared directly in front of me. He asked, "Do you believe that I can walk on the water?" Then I remembered from the Scriptures that He had walked on the water and that Peter had stepped out of the boat to meet Him. I said, "Yes, I believe you can walk on the water."

Then Jesus said, "Since you believe, then take my arm and walk beside Me as we cross over to the other side."

I committed myself to Him in total trust. We locked arms and began to cross the river. I kept my eyes closed and held on tightly because I did not want to doubt and sink like Peter did as he viewed his circumstances.

After we made it across, Jesus was gone, but other people appeared. They were taking pictures and putting microphones up to my mouth. They reminded me of news reporters. They inquired about my ability to walk on water — how was it possible?

"I didn't do it myself. Jesus was with me. I only did what He told me. I held on, trusted, and stepped out." The crowd continued snapping pictures and gathering around me.

After I woke up the next day, I knew God gave me the dream for a reason. I prayed for the interpretation. He showed me that as long as I kept my eyes on Him and remained totally committed, without wavering and fearing the circumstances around me, He would see me through. I was to be faithful and trusting of Him. Whether I could feel Him with me or not, He assured me that He was always there beside me. Hebrews 13:5 says, "He will never leave me nor forsake me." No matter what obstacle I come against, I can overcome with Him. Through this dream, my faith increased even more and I realized there were four areas in my life that were crucial in my walk with God: commitment, obedience, faithfulness, and discipline.

One month later, Larry and I went to a weekend Women's Aglow Retreat in Brown Country, Indiana. One afternoon, during a time of worshiping the Lord, Larry cried out for God to use us that we might bring Him glory. Larry looked at me with tears in his eyes and said, "Is the Lord saying the same thing to you?"

"Yes," I wept.

It was beautiful to see how God spoke to both of us at the same time to commit ourselves to Him one hundred percent, forsaking anything that would hold us back.

To think of surrendering everything to God was a bit scary. We were to step out and walk on the water. We did not know what God had in store for us, nor where we were headed, but one thing we did know, there was a calling of God upon our lives.

What kind of ministry were we to enter into? A Korean/American ministry seemed logical. All we knew to do was to fast and pray and seek God's direction. We held on to the Scripture in Isaiah 55:8 and 9: "For my thoughts are not your thoughts, neither are your ways my ways. As the heavens are higher than the earth, so are my ways higher than your ways and my thoughts than your thoughts."

On April 21, 1981, Larry told our pastor that we felt God's call on our lives. We knew we were to wait on God, so with the pastor's blessing, we left the church. Through God's direction we began a home church meeting. On Sunday mornings and Wednesday evenings we had home meetings — just the five of us. Through this time we became a closer family, establishing God's order in our home.

The Lord delivered me from witchcraft during this time. As a youngster I went to a fortune teller to inquire about my future. She told me that one day I would die because of female problems. Whenever I had the slightest pain, fear gripped me as I would recall her words. Try as I did, I could not shake off the fear and anxiety this suggestion carried with it.

One night, as I was suffering from terrible cramps, I shared the story of my visit to the fortune teller with Larry.

"Why haven't you shared this before? Asking advice from a fortune teller is asking ungodly counsel, Sun. She fed you a lie and tried to place a curse on you. Don't receive her words. Wasn't your mom deeply involved at one time with them, too? Let's get Mama Lee and pray about this. There's no reason for you to live under such tormenting fear," he reassured me.

The three of us prayed together. In every way we could think of in which we had opened the door to the satanic presence in our lives, we repented and renounced what we had done many years ago. I have been free of this fear ever since.

As time went on, I found myself praying, "Lord, have we missed you? Have we made a mistake? It seems we are in a wilderness. I miss the fellowship with the brethren so much. You are going to have to show me whether or not we've missed you."

We spent thirty days praying and seeking God's direction. I was reminded of one of my past dreams where Larry and I spent time doing just what we had been doing — seeking God's direction. In the dream we continued praying, but were interrupted by people knocking on our door who were asking to join us.

On May 30, a brother in the Lord called and asked if he could bring his family over to our home the following morning to spend some time in prayer with us. We were glad to have them join us. We had come out of the wilderness after these thirty days of prayer.

Then the next week, on Sunday morning, they joined us again. The third week we got together and shared the Scriptures and prayed for one another. A week later, another family came to join us for prayer and sharing.

Later, on Thursday nights, we began having meetings. As the weeks passed Larry began teaching on Sunday mornings and Thursday nights.

The Lord told us that He was going to bring people to our door: the broken-hearted, the lost sheep, the rejected, and people who had lost their way. Ezekiel 34 tells about the type of people who came to us: the spiritually lost, the weak and the sick, the injured and bound.

As leaders, we became responsible for the flock. In August, 1981, I had a dream of a cross in the sky; from this a fireball came to the ground. The dry grass and dead trees which I saw in the dream were engulfed by flames, but not consumed. People came to me to tell me that my house was on fire. Startled, I awoke.

The following Thursday evening, I shared my dream with our prayer group. We all felt the cross represented Jesus, and the fire was the Holy Spirit. Acts 2 tells of the tongues of fire on the heads of men who were filled with the Holy Spirit. The grass represented dry hearts and the trees were representative of the dead souls, for the trees had no life, nor did they bear fruit. They needed the Spirit of God to come down and touch them and bring life to their souls. Seeing my house on fire, I knew the Holy Spirit was moving in our home.

16

About My Father's Business

In September we opened our home for anyone who wanted to come for church services. We set up many chairs in the living room. Before long, each service was packed. I recalled one of my dreams where people came to our home, but the living room could not contain everyone. My dreams were coming to pass. We used the bedrooms and the garage for Sunday school rooms. "Lord, we need more space. Even though our living room and garage are big, we need to have our meetings elsewhere," I prayed.

In November, 1981, we were incorporated and are now the Body of Christ Fellowship. We have a vision to be the visible expression of the Body of Christ in His love, authority and power with each individual member fulfilling his ministry as a member of this body. It is our vision to be ministering unto the Lord in worship; unto one another in service; and unto the world in evangelization. Our purpose is to equip each member to do the work of the ministry through the teaching of the Word, providing a climate of love, acceptance and forgiveness, and leading each one to submit to the Lordship of Jesus Christ. We believe that it is the Lord's desire for each member to reach his full potential of growth, "unto the measure of the stature of the fullness of Christ."

We were able to move into a building in Greenfield that was used for community services. We were thrilled with our new location that enabled us to stretch out. There were one hundred chairs, a blackboard for teaching, a kitchen, heat and air-conditioning. It was perfect, so we met there, rent-free, on Sunday mornings. On Thursday nights, we continued meeting in our home.

As people gave their tithes and offerings, we were able to help those in need. We were also able to save some money in order to rent our own place.

In May of 1982, we moved into rooms above a downtown business. We had a dedication service for our new location. There was great rejoicing among all the people.

As our fellowship began to grow, I battled with insecurity again. Originally we thought we would work with a Korean/American congregation. I felt I was not good enough to be a pastor's wife to Americans. I did not feel I could talk or pray as well as others. This really bothered me. Larry kept encouraging me that I was needed and that I was an asset.

"Honey, if God wanted you to be an American then He would have made you one. You need to accept yourself for who you are and quit comparing yourself to other Americans. God made you Korean because He wants you to be one. You are unique and very special —irreplaceable."

The Scripture in Jeremiah 1:5 brought life to me. The NIV Bible says, "Before I formed you in the womb I knew you, before you were born I set you apart; I appointed you as a prophet to the nations." Before we were born, God knew us and called us.

Through dreams, the studying of God's Word, and through Larry, God comforted me and helped me to grow more secure in Him. However, rejection would again become a battle for me. A lady in our fellowship seemed to be uncomfortable around me. I loved her, but I could not break through the wall I felt between us. Dee wrote me a letter one day, asking if we could sing a certain song about loving one another, but she went on to say that she and I did not seem to have the love and unity. "Wait a minute," I thought. "She knows I love her and would do anything for her." Then, I realized why I felt a wall between us. I decided to go to Dee to reassure her of my love. I had no bad feelings towards her at all.

I went to her home. I told Dee I loved her and would do anything to make our relationship right. She became upset and felt I was not being honest with her. "Well, Dee," I pled, "What can I do? Why do you think I'm not being honest?"

"I don't think you're being yourself. You act phony. You always seem so happy and you hug and love on people so much. It's impossible for people to act like that, realistically," she contended.

With the situation unresolved, I left the house with my heart bruised. I thought I would drop her because she had rejected me. The Lord dealt with me by pointing out that if I truly loved her, I should not do that. He wanted me to continue to show my love to her. As time passed, the wall seemed to thicken between us. Rejection started to rise up within me. I was the one who called her. She never called me unless it had to do with church-related business. I grew tired of always being the one to reach out to Dee. I told the Lord that I was sick and tired of putting out the effort. I planned to ignore her the following Sunday.

On Sunday, I did not speak to her or even acknowledge her presence. When I got home, I felt miserable for deliberately ignoring her. I asked God what He would have me do. He quickly reminded me of First John 3:16: "This is how we know what love is: Jesus laid down his life for us. And we ought to lay down our lives for our brothers" (*NIV*). He reminded me that He loved me so much that He died for me. Then I felt so bad for going about it my way instead of God's way. I was quick to repent and was determined to love her unconditionally, free from the fear of rejection. Praise God for His faithfulness to meet our every need.

Before I came to know the Lord, I was a very stubborn person who was full of bitterness and retaliation. Since I have entered into a precious relationship with Jesus, He is using that stubborn nature for my benefit and His glory. I am a very determined person in serving God. Now when a hardship confronts me, I am diligent to go God's way and trust Him. When necessary, I persevere and persist in what I know is right and God-pleasing. I am not swayed by people's opinions and words to influence me to do wrong. I am eternally grateful for what God had done in my life and for changing me.

When the company I worked for shut down in May, 1984, and moved out-of-state, I was so relieved and grateful. With my life busy at home and active in church, I felt I was burning from both ends. I needed to be free to help people full-time and be available when needed.

Soon afterwards, I returned to Korea to spend time with my family. I was able to share the Lord with them. When they saw how God had changed me, the Holy Spirit touched their hearts. Fifteen family members gave up serving Buddha, and are now serving the living God. I visited Dr. Paul Yonggi Cho's huge church and spent time fasting and praying on Prayer Mountain, which is internationally known.

Several years before my trip to Korea, I felt strongly impressed to one day publish a book about my life story. As the Lord directed me, I wrote a book in Korean. The book would be able to touch so many people who need to know about a living God who loves, forgives and changes people like me. While in Korea, I saw Pastor Lee who used to pastor the Korean church in Indianapolis. He was so thrilled about my testimony that he offered to help sponsor me financially to get the book published.

There was also a professional writer who was willing to rewrite my story. With great excitement, I called home to tell Larry the wonderful news. From the tone of his voice I could tell he really missed me and needed me back home. I had already been gone a month and a half. After I told him I would be gone for three or four months more to oversee the book, he grew very quiet. Larry felt that I needed to come home and be with him and the children. Although I wanted so much to have my story published, I knew my family had priority over my book, so I came home.

Although disappointed because my book was not published while in Korea, I was filled with a burning desire to fast and pray to know God more intimately and to pray for America's salvation.

This desire was birthed in my spirit while I was at Prayer Mountain. A new relationship was formed between God and me. I used to seek riches and love before Jesus. Now Jesus had satisfied my every longing and he had made me a new person. This deeper relationship between God and me has changed my life again. I now have complete freedom from all my emotional problems, fear, insecurity, rejection, hatred, bitterness. I have found that the Christian life is not boring or miserable. On the contrary, my life is so busy and exciting. As God showed me in a dream in 1984, I traveled and shared God's love in women's groups and churches in many places. God continues to use Larry and me in ministering to others through prayer and counseling. We have seen such beautiful results and answered prayers in the lives of people.

The Body of Christ Fellowship has purchased its own building on U.S. Highway 40, east of Greenfield. We are so grateful to have our own place to worship the Lord and learn His Word so we can help meet the needs of others. God has met the desires of my heart as He promised He would do in Psalms 37:4: (NIV) "Delight

yourself in the Lord and He will give you the desires of
your heart." If your desire is to be free from the life you
now live and you sense an emptiness inside that nothing
has been able to satisfy, I want you to know that the living
God, Jesus Christ, is the One who can change and satisfy
your life."

Because Larry and I are so busy, mother deserves a
great big thank-you from the two of us. She is a beautiful
servant of the Lord. She has given so much of herself by
taking care of the boys and doing domestic chores. My
family loves her and appreciates all her generosity and
sacrifices for us. I know it has not been easy for her, at
times, because she does not speak fluent English.

Before closing, I want to thank the Lord for working out
the many details, as my heart's desire has been fulfilled in
the writing of my book. Susan Engle and I spent many
hours together as I shared my life's story with her. God had
His perfect time. "All things work together for the good to
those who love Him" (Rom. 8:28).

*If we confess our sins, he is faithful and just and will
forgive us our sins and purify us from all unrighteous-
ness. (I John 1:9).*

*"Call to me and I will answer you and tell you great and
unsearchable things you do not know. (Jer. 33:3).*

If you have felt the Lord wooing your heart to Him as
you have read this book, then please pray with me:

*Lord, I am not fully satisfied with the way I have led
my life, so I ask for you to lead me. Forgive me for all
the things I have done and said and thought which
grieved and displeased you. I know I have not lived in*

obedience to you, but I would like to do so now. Cleanse me in the blood of Jesus and mold me into the person you created me to be. I open my heart to you. Come in and fill the empty void inside. I welcome you, Lord Jesus, into my life. In Jesus' Name I pray. Amen.

Epilogue

God's goodness and faithfulness never cease to amaze me. He is faithful in keeping His promises to us, and He never fails. Experiencing this reality and knowing all that He has done for me, my heart's desire and prayer has been for Him to manifest Himself through me. I have desired and continue to desire that Christ be exalted in my body. The Scripture I have claimed is Philippians 1:20-21 (TLB): "I eagerly expect and hope that I will in no way be ashamed, but will have sufficient courage so that now as always Christ will be exalted in my body, whether by life of by death. For to me, to live is Christ and to die is gain."

Knowing that in my flesh there dwells no good thing, I cried out to God, yearning to be like Jesus. I cried out, "Lord, if there is anything in me that is displeasing to you, then show me." He dealt with me concerning three areas in my life that needed His touch. The first area was that I allowed myself to limit my vision and be satisfied with ministering in my own local church. God was calling me to deeper waters, to increase my vision and to take off the limits so that He could use me in a bigger way. He was calling me to reach out to multitudes and be used in ways I never thought possible. He showed me that there would be a cost involved — more of Him and less of me. I had to enter into the crucified life and give Him my all.

The second area was that I participated in works of the flesh. I found myself occupied with activities of the church, visiting people, and going here and there. All these things were good, but I needed to seek the Lord and depend on Him to show me the direction to take and what to do. He taught me the true meaning of Revelations 2:2-5, (*NIV*): "I know your deeds, your hard work and your perseverance. I know that you cannot tolerate wicked men, that you have tested those who claim to be apostles but are not and have found them false. You have persevered and have endured hardships for my name, and have not grown weary. Yet, I hold this against you: You have forsaken you first love. Remember the height from which you have fallen! Repent and do the things you did at first. If you do not repent, I will come to you and remove your lampstand from its place." We can get so easily into our own fleshly works instead of waiting on God. I was doing all these works out of duty instead of taking time to seek Him. I had in the course of all my "duties" left my first love. I got so involved with duties that often I would get ahead of Him. At times He wanted me to pray for the needs of others and instead I was trying to meet those needs myself.

Thirdly, one day as I was fasting, God showed me that I needed to repent of pride and self-righteousness. When God showed me that I was wrong in these areas, I did not want to admit it. I tried to justify myself. This attitude was hindering my spiritual growth. I sought God's mercy and forgiveness, which He freely granted. As a loving Father, God is faithful to instruct His beloved children when He sees them turn to the left or to the right of His perfect plan designed for them. He graciously showed me what I needed to change. For ten days, I fasted and prayed for God to change me and cleanse me. I wanted to go from glory to glory and conform to His image. My heart greatly yearned for, and my mind was consumed with, the desire to be changed from within. But the struggle that took place in my heart caused me to cry uncontrollably for two and a half days. I sobbed and sobbed, desiring to change, but at the same time struggling to let that change occur. I was so hurt at the ugliness that was revealed in me that I felt as if my heart was torn in two. I knew I needed to change but at the same time it was so hard to admit it. But, praise God, the breakthrough came and I had victory as I yielded to the transforming work of the Holy Spirit.

After fasting for ten days, the Lord gave me a burden for the Koreans and the Americans in the local area to unite together for a time of prayer and fasting for revival. He impressed upon my heart to pray for one hundred days. During this period of time in May of 1986, I met Betty Green for the first time. Betty is the president of the American Prayer Mountain and the American represen-tative to the Korean Prayer Mountain which is a mountain where Christians meet to fast and pray in small cubicles built within the mountain slopes. Immediately, Betty held my interest, for I clung to her every word as she shared of her experiences with Dr. Jashil Choi, the founder and director of "Haven of Prayer," Prayer Mountain, in Seoul, Korea.

Dr. Choi is the mother-in-law of the highly recognized pastor of the Yoido Full Gospel Church in Seoul, Korea, Dr. Paul Yonggi Cho. The current membership of this church is 500,000. Besides her ministry at Prayer Mountain, Dr. Choi has ministered in ten countries, became an ordained minister in Japan, and in 1974, she received an honorary Doctor of Divinity Degree from the ministry of Yoido Full Gospel Church. But she continues to travel and assist churches in starting a strong prayer ministry. Dr. Choi was also the Korean representative to a national meeting concerning prayer in America conducted by President Reagan. Betty promised me that Dr. Choi would be able to speak at our church the following September. Words could not describe my excitement and joy. The thought of Dr. Choi coming to Greenfield was like a dream!

During the month of June, 1986, I began a thirty-day fast with three goals in mind. The first was to attain more power of God in my personal walk and ministry. Second was the burning desire within my heart for revival in our church and among the Koreans in the local vicinity. Third was to write a book of my life story in English. On the third day of the fast, God gave me a woman, Susan K. Engle, to write my book. On the seventh day of my fast, a Pastor Gary Bloom called from Spencer, Indiana, to inform me that he had some land he would like to be used for a Prayer Mountain in this state. I was amazed how everything was working out so beautifully. Also, with each passing day, I was growing in God's grace and power.

As Betty promised, Dr. Choi arrived in September for three nights of speaking engagements to both Koreans and Americans. To be a part of this unity and revival was such a blessing. God truly answered my prayer in bringing the local Koreans and Americans together in prayer and worship in perfect love and unity. God opened doors that no man can shut.

During this time, I was deeply touched by the Koreans who came to me asking for forgiveness. In the past, it was difficult for many of them to accept me for marrying an American man who had divorced a Korean woman. The

Koreans are very loyal to their people. Also, Larry and I were ministering as pastor without credentials from a Bible school. That was unacceptable to them. According to their standards, we are not qualified to stand in the leadership position we were holding. But, praise the Lord, the Holy Spirit has been my teacher, instructing me though the years. As I remain in the Vine and tap into the main Source of power, the Holy Spirit teaches me His Word.

Now that the Lord has brought a healing between the Korean brethren and myself, I walk in greater freedom to attain my new vision. My vision is to one day minister, alongside my husband, to the Korean and American couples who have been discriminated against in their mixed marriages. Also, I desire to see Prayer Mountain established in Indiana. With man it's impossible, but with God all things are possible.

After all, the one who was called "Bad-Luck Baby" has become a child of God who receives His abundant blessings and love. Could anyone ask for a greater miracle than that?

Through the years I have experienced inner healing for different parts of my life. Recently I was healed from the wound of aborting my unborn child many years ago. Until recently I was not conscious of my having been hurt by the abortion. I was not aware that it was the same as committing murder, because the acceptance of abortion as being the right thing is widespread in Korean society. I just thought the decision was an unfortunate one.

I knew God had forgiven me for all my sins, but for some reason I could not think or talk about my abortion. I always had uneasy feelings about what I had done to my baby and, whenever these thoughts came to me, I always told Satan, "Back-off!' It is all under the blood and God has forgiven me. I will not receive your guilt and condemnation!" I continued suppressing these thoughts and refused to share this part of my life in my ministering to others.

The realization that I had murdered my baby came the day I could not bear to look at the pictures of aborted babies. The sight was devastating and heartbreaking because the pictures reminded me of what had happened years ago. I asked God why I was so devastated. Then God let me feel the hurt and pain that my baby felt. I finally realized I had to face the reality that I needed a healing in this area of my life. For the first time I could admit to God that I had murdered my baby and I cried out to God for mercy and forgiveness. I always felt sorry for what had happened but I could not recall that I ever felt sorry for my baby because of the fact that I did not allow him to be born to live.

I cried and cried for a whole week. I needed to grieve for my baby and to forgive myself and to release the guilt and shame to God. I yearned for relief within my soul and peace of mind. Through an act of my will I forgave myself and received God's freedom from guilt.

Ever since my healing of abortion, God has opened many doors of ministry to other women who have experienced abortions, wounds and suffering.

"Praise be to the God and Father of our Lord Jesus Christ, the Father of compassion and the God of all comfort, who comforts us in all our troubles, so that we can comfort those in any trouble with the comfort we ourselves have received from God. For just as the sufferings of Christ flow over into our lives, so also through Christ our comfort overflows." (2 Cor. 1:3-5).

For ordering testimony tapes, books, or for speaking engagements, please call 317-326-8658 or write to 106 Cranberry Drive, Greenfield, IN 46140